THE AUSTRALIAN
Women's Weekly
little squares & slices

acp
books

The oven temperatures in this book are for conventional ovens; if you have a fan-forced oven, decrease the temperature by 10-20 degrees.

dark chocolate and nougat fudge bars

360g (11½ ounces) dark eating (semi-sweet) chocolate, chopped coarsely
395g (12½ ounces) canned sweetened condensed milk
30g (1 ounce) butter
200g (6½ ounces) soft nougat, chopped coarsely

1 Grease 20cm x 30cm (8-inch x 12-inch) rectangular pan; line base and long sides with baking paper, extending paper 5cm (2 inches) over sides.
2 Combine chocolate, condensed milk and butter in large saucepan; stir over low heat until smooth. Remove from heat; stir in nougat. Pour mixture into pan, smooth surface with a wet spatula. Refrigerate about 3 hours or until firm before cutting.

prep + cook time 15 minutes (+ refrigeration)
makes 96
Store bars in an airtight container in the fridge for up to a week, or freeze for up to four weeks.

caramel &
butterscotch

popcorn butterscotch squares

250g (8 ounces) butternut snap biscuits
125g (4 ounces) butter, melted
395g (12½ ounces) canned sweetened condensed milk
30g (1 ounce) butter, extra
4 cups (40g) air-popped salted popcorn
½ cup (40g) toasted shredded coconut
185g (6 ounces) milk eating chocolate, melted

1 Grease 20cm x 30cm (8-inch x 12-inch) rectangular pan; line base and long sides with baking paper, extending paper 5cm (2 inches) over sides.
2 Process biscuits until fine. Add butter; process until combined. Press mixture firmly over base of pan. Refrigerate 30 minutes or until firm.
3 Meanwhile, combine condensed milk and extra butter in medium heavy-based saucepan; cook, stirring, over medium heat, about 10 minutes or until mixture is a caramel colour. Remove from heat; quickly stir in the popcorn and coconut.
4 Working quickly with wet hands, spread and firmly press popcorn mixture over base. Spread chocolate over slice. Refrigerate about 30 minutes or until set before cutting.

prep + cook time 30 minutes (+ refrigeration)
makes 24
Store squares in an airtight container in the fridge for up to 4 days.

contents

fig and chocolate caramel slice

125g (4 ounces) butter
1 cup (220g) firmly packed light brown sugar
1¼ cups (135g) coarsely chopped dried figs
1 egg, beaten lightly
¾ cup (110g) self-raising flour
¼ cup (25g) cocoa powder

1 Preheat oven to 180°C/350°F. Grease 20cm x 30cm (8-inch x 12-inch) rectangular pan; line base and long sides with baking paper, extending paper 5cm (2 inches) over sides.
2 Melt butter in medium saucepan over medium heat; stir in sugar until dissolved. Remove from heat; stand 5 minutes. Stir in figs, then egg and sifted flour and cocoa. Press mixture into pan.
3 Bake about 15 minutes. Cool slice in pan before cutting into pieces.

prep + cook time 25 minutes
makes 25
Store slice in an airtight container for up to a week.

salted caramel chocolate slice

125g (4 ounces) butter, chopped coarsely
155g (5 ounces) dark eating (semi-sweet)
   chocolate, chopped coarsely
1 egg
⅔ (150g) caster (superfine) sugar
¾ cup (110g) plain (all-purpose) flour
¼ cup (35g) self-raising flour
salted caramel filling
395g (12½ ounces) canned sweetened
   condensed milk
30g (1 ounce) butter
¼ cup (90g) golden syrup or treacle
2 teaspoons coarse cooking salt (kosher salt)
chocolate glaze
185g (6 ounces) dark eating (semi-sweet)
   chocolate, chopped coarsely
50g (1½ ounces) butter

1 Preheat oven to 180°C/350°F. Grease 20cm x 30cm (8-inch x 12-inch) rectangular pan; line base and long sides with baking paper, extending paper 5cm (2 inches) over sides.
2 Stir butter and chocolate in medium saucepan over low heat until smooth. Cool.
3 Beat egg and sugar in small bowl with electric mixer until thick and creamy. Stir in chocolate mixture and sifted flours. Spread mixture into pan; bake 10 minutes. Remove from oven.
4 Meanwhile, make salted caramel filling.
5 Pour filling over chocolate base; smooth surface with spatula. Bake 8 minutes. Cool slice 10 minutes; refrigerate until cold.
6 Make chocolate glaze; spread over caramel. Refrigerate about 2 hours or until set before cutting.

salted caramel filling Stir ingredients in small saucepan over medium heat about 12 minutes or until mixture thickens and becomes caramel in colour.

chocolate glaze Stir ingredients in small saucepan over low heat until smooth.

prep + cook time 40 minutes (+ refrigeration)
makes 40
tip To achieve a smooth chocolate glaze, spread the glaze over the slice with a spatula, then tap the pan gently on the bench until the glaze becomes smooth.
Store slice in an airtight container in the fridge for up to 2 weeks.

caramel, honey and cashew slice

2½ cups (375g) roasted salted cashews
⅓ cup (50g) plain (all-purpose) flour
¼ cup (55g) firmly packed light brown sugar
45g (1½ ounces) butter, melted
3 eggs
¼ cup (90g) honey
1 tablespoon honey, extra, warmed
pastry
1 cup (150g) plain (all-purpose) flour
¼ cup (40g) icing (confectioners') sugar
100g (3 ounces) cold butter, chopped coarsely
1 egg yolk
1 teaspoon iced water, approximately

1 Make pastry.
2 Grease 20cm x 30cm (8-inch x 12-inch) rectangular pan; line base and long sides with baking paper, extending paper 5cm (2 inches) over sides.
3 Roll pastry between sheets of baking paper until large enough to line base of pan. Lift pastry into pan; trim excess. Refrigerate 30 minutes.
4 Preheat oven to 180°C/350°F.
5 Bake pastry base 10 minutes; cool.
6 Reduce oven temperature to 160°C/325°F.
7 Combine nuts, flour, sugar, butter, eggs and honey in medium bowl. Pour mixture over base. Bake about 40 minutes; cool. Brush slice with extra honey before cutting.

pastry Process flour, icing sugar and butter until crumbly. Add egg yolk and enough of the water to make ingredients come together. Knead dough on floured surface until smooth.

prep + cook time 1 hour (+ refrigeration)
makes 30
Store slice in an airtight container for up to 3 days.

classic chocolate caramel slice

1 cup (150g) plain (all-purpose) flour
½ cup (110g) firmly packed light brown sugar
½ cup (40g) desiccated coconut
125g (4 ounces) butter, melted
60g (2 ounces) butter, extra
395g (12½ ounces) canned sweetened
   condensed milk
2 tablespoons golden syrup or treacle
185g (6 ounces) dark eating (semi-sweet)
   chocolate, chopped coarsely
2 teaspoons vegetable oil

1 Preheat oven to 180°C/350°F. Grease 20cm x 30cm (8-inch x 12-inch) rectangular pan; line base and long sides with baking paper, extending paper 5cm (2 inches) over sides.
2 Combine sifted flour, sugar and coconut in medium bowl; stir in butter. Press flour mixture firmly into pan; bake about 15 minutes. Cool.
3 Combine extra butter, condensed milk and syrup in medium saucepan; stir over low heat until smooth. Pour mixture over base. Bake about 15 minutes or until golden brown. Cool.
4 Stir chocolate and oil in medium heatproof bowl over medium saucepan of simmering water until smooth. Spread chocolate mixture over slice. Refrigerate about 30 minutes or until set before cutting slice using a hot knife.

prep + cook time 55 minutes (+ refrigeration)
makes 48
Store slice in an airtight container for up to a week.

sticky date slice

1⅓ cups (185g) coarsely chopped seeded
  dried dates
1⅓ cups (330ml) water
½ teaspoon bicarbonate of soda (baking soda)
60g (2 ounces) butter, softened
¾ cup (165g) firmly packed light brown sugar
2 eggs
1 cup (150g) self-raising flour
caramel topping
½ cup (110g) firmly packed light brown sugar
2 tablespoons water
20g (¾ ounce) butter
1 tablespoon golden syrup or treacle
1 cup (250ml) thickened (heavy) cream

1 Preheat oven to 180°C/350°F. Grease 24cm x 32cm (9½-inch x 13-inch) swiss roll pan; line base and long sides with baking paper, extending paper 5cm (2 inches) over sides.
2 Combine dates and the water in medium saucepan; bring to the boil. Remove from heat; stir in soda, stand 5 minutes.
3 Meanwhile, beat butter and sugar in medium bowl with electric mixer until light and fluffy; beat in eggs, one at a time. Stir in sifted flour, then date mixture. Pour mixture into pan. Bake about 20 minutes. Cool slice in pan.
4 Make caramel topping.
5 Cut slice into squares; top each square with a dollop of caramel topping. Sprinkle with chocolate curls, if you like.

caramel topping Stir sugar and the water in small saucepan, over low heat, until sugar dissolves. Bring to the boil; boil, uncovered, 4 minutes. Remove from heat; stir in butter and syrup. Transfer mixture to small bowl; add ¼ cup (60ml) of the cream. Beat with electric mixer until thickened slightly; cool. Beat remaining cream in small bowl with electric mixer until soft peaks form; beat in caramel mixture until firm peaks form. Refrigerate until required.

prep + cook time 40 minutes (+ cooling)
makes 12
Store slice in an airtight container in the fridge for up to 3 days.

banoffee slice

1 cup (150g) self-raising flour
¼ cup (55g) caster (superfine) sugar
100g (3½ ounces) butter, melted
2 medium bananas (400g), sliced thinly diagonally
1 cup (250ml) thickened (heavy) cream, whipped
60g (2 ounces) milk eating chocolate

caramel filling

395g (12½ ounces) canned sweetened
    condensed milk
90g (3 ounces) butter, chopped coarsely
½ cup (110g) firmly packed light brown sugar
2 tablespoons golden syrup or treacle

1 Preheat oven to 180°C/350°F. Grease 20cm x 30cm (8-inch x 12-inch) rectangular pan; line base and long sides with baking paper, extending paper 5cm (2 inches) over sides.

2 Combine sifted flour and sugar in small bowl; stir in butter. Press mixture firmly over base of pan. Bake about 20 minutes. Cool.

3 Meanwhile, make the caramel filling.

4 Pour filling over base. Refrigerate 1 hour or until firm.

5 Place banana over caramel; top with whipped cream. Grate chocolate, using a vegetable peeler; sprinkle over cream before cutting slice.

caramel filling Stir ingredients in medium saucepan over medium heat about 12 minutes or until caramel in colour. Cool 5 minutes.

prep + cook time 45 minutes (+ refrigeration)
makes 30
Slice is best eaten on the day it is made, however, it can be stored in an airtight container in the fridge for up to 2 days.

toffee apple slice

¾ cup (110g) potato flour
¾ cup (120g) brown rice flour
1 teaspoon bicarbonate of soda (baking soda)
1 cup (220g) firmly packed light brown sugar
3 medium apples (450g), peeled, cored,
   grated coarsely
3 eggs
¾ cup (180ml) vegetable oil
walnut praline
¾ cup (165g) caster (superfine) sugar
2 tablespoons water
½ cup (55g) finely chopped roasted walnuts
apple icing
2 cups (320g) pure icing (confectioners') sugar
¼ cup (60ml) apple juice, approximately

1 Preheat oven to 180°C/350°F. Grease 24cm x 32cm (9½-inch x 13-inch) swiss roll pan; line base and long sides with baking paper, extending paper 5cm (2 inches) over sides.
2 Sift dry ingredients into large bowl; stir in apple, eggs and oil. Pour mixture into pan; bake about 30 minutes. Stand slice in pan 10 minutes, before turning, top-side up, onto wire rack to cool.
3 Meanwhile, make the walnut praline topping.
4 Make apple icing. Spread slice with icing; sprinkle with praline before cutting

walnut praline Combine sugar and the water in small saucepan; stir over low heat until sugar dissolves. Bring to the boil; boil, uncovered, without stirring, about 10 minutes or until toffee is a caramel colour. Remove from heat; allow bubbles to subside. Place nuts in single layer on baking-paper-lined oven tray; pour toffee all over nuts. Stand at room temperature until set. Chop praline finely.

apple icing Sift icing sugar into small bowl; stir in enough juice to make a thick paste. Set bowl over small saucepan of simmering water; stir icing until spreadable.

prep + cook time 1 hour (+ standing)
makes 30
note This recipe works like an impossible pie; it separates into layers during cooking.
Slice is best eaten on the day it is made.

caramel coconut macaroon slice

90g (3 ounces) unsalted butter, softened
½ cup (110g) caster (superfine) sugar
1 egg
⅔ cup (100g) plain (all-purpose) flour
⅓ cup (50g) self-raising flour
caramel coconut topping
3 eggs, beaten lightly
¼ cup (60ml) milk
60g (2 ounces) unsalted butter, melted, cooled
1 teaspoon coconut essence
1¼ cups (275g) firmly packed light brown sugar
2 cups (150g) shredded coconut

1 Preheat oven to 160°C/325°F. Grease 20cm x 30cm
(8-inch x 12-inch) rectangular pan; line base and
long sides with baking paper, extending paper 5cm
(2 inches) over sides.
2 Beat butter, sugar and egg in small bowl with
electric mixer until light and fluffy; stir in sifted flours.
Spread mixture into pan; refrigerate 20 minutes.
3 Meanwhile, make caramel coconut topping.
4 Pour topping over base. Bake about 45 minutes.
Cool slice in pan, before cutting.

caramel coconut topping Combine ingredients in
medium bowl.

prep + cook time 1 hour (+ refrigeration)
makes 30
Store slice in an airtight container for up to 4 days.
Use a serrated knife to cut this slice.

honey nut squares

125g (4 ounces) unsalted butter, softened
½ cup (110g) caster (superfine) sugar
1 egg yolk
1 cup (150g) plain (all-purpose) flour
⅓ cup (50g) self-raising flour
⅔ cup (240g) honey
⅓ cup (75g) firmly packed light brown sugar
90g (3 ounces) unsalted butter, chopped coarsely
2 tablespoons thickened (heavy) cream
1 cup (120g) pecans
½ cup (80g) almond kernels
½ cup (70g) roasted hazelnuts

1 Preheat oven to 160°C/325°F. Grease 20cm x 30cm (8-inch x 12-inch) rectangular pan; line base and long sides with baking paper, extending paper 5cm (2 inches) over sides.
2 Beat softened butter, caster sugar and egg yolk in small bowl with electric mixer until light and fluffy. Stir in sifted flours. Press mixture evenly over base of pan. Bake 15 minutes.
3 Stir honey, brown sugar and chopped butter in medium saucepan over low heat until sugar is dissolved. Bring to the boil; boil, uncovered, without stirring, 2 minutes. Add cream; boil, stirring, 1 minute. Remove from heat. Stir in nuts until coated in caramel mixture. Working quickly, pour nut mixture over base; spread evenly with spatula.
4 Bake about 15 minutes. Cool slice in pan. Refrigerate 2 hours before cutting.

prep + cook time 50 minutes (+ refrigeration)
makes 35
Store squares in an airtight container for up to 4 days.

millionaire's shortbread

125g (4 ounces) unsalted butter, softened
½ cup (110g) caster (superfine) sugar
1 egg yolk
1 cup (150g) plain (all-purpose) flour
⅓ cup (50g) self-raising flour
395g (12½ ounces) canned sweetened
 condensed milk
30g (1 ounce) unsalted butter, extra
2 tablespoons golden syrup or treacle
1 cup (140g) roasted salted peanuts
200g (6½ ounces) milk eating chocolate,
 chopped coarsely
2 teaspoons vegetable oil

1 Preheat oven to 160°C/325°F. Grease 20cm x 30cm (8-inch x 12-inch) rectangular pan; line base and long sides with baking paper, extending paper 5cm (2 inches) over sides.
2 Beat butter, sugar and egg yolk in small bowl with electric mixer until light and fluffy. Stir in sifted flours. Press mixture evenly over base of pan. Bake 15 minutes.
3 Meanwhile, stir condensed milk, extra butter and syrup in small saucepan, over medium heat, about 15 minutes or until mixture is golden brown. Working quickly, pour caramel over base; smooth surface with spatula. Press peanuts into caramel with spatula. Bake 10 minutes; cool.
4 Stir chocolate and oil in small saucepan over low heat until smooth. Pour chocolate mixture over caramel. Refrigerate about 2 hours or until set before cutting.

prep + cook time 50 minutes (+ refrigeration)
makes 40
Store in an airtight container for up to 3 days.

white chocolate caramel slice

⅓ cup (30g) rolled oats
½ cup (75g) self-raising flour
2 teaspoons cocoa powder
⅓ cup (75g) firmly packed light brown sugar
½ cup (40g) desiccated coconut
90g (3 ounces) butter, melted
395g (12½ ounces) canned sweetened
    condensed milk
⅓ cup (115g) golden syrup or treacle
30g (1 ounce) butter, chopped coarsely
250g (6½ ounces) white eating chocolate,
    chopped coarsely
2 teaspoons vegetable oil

1 Preheat oven to 180°C/350°F. Grease 20cm x 30cm (8-inch x 12-inch) rectangular pan; line base and long sides with baking paper, extending paper 5cm (2 inches) over sides.
2 Process oats until finely chopped. Combine oats with sifted flour and cocoa in medium bowl. Stir in sugar, coconut and melted butter. Press mixture evenly over base of pan. Bake 10 minutes.
3 Combine condensed milk, syrup and chopped butter in small saucepan. Bring to the boil, stirring, about 5 minutes or until thickened. Pour mixture over base. Bake 10 minutes. Cool.
4 Stir chocolate and oil in small heatproof bowl over small saucepan of simmering water until smooth; spread over caramel. Refrigerate about 30 minutes or until set before cutting slice using a hot knife.

prep + cook time 45 minutes (+ refrigeration)
makes 20
Store slice in an airtight container in the fridge for up to 4 days.

caramel apple squares

1 sheet butter puff pastry
125g (4 ounces) unsalted butter, softened
½ cup (110g) caster (superfine) sugar
2 eggs
¾ cup (90g) ground almonds
¼ cup (35g) plain (all-purpose) flour
1 teaspoon finely grated lemon rind
caramel apples
60g (2 ounces) unsalted butter
⅓ cup (75g) raw sugar
3 medium apples (450g), peeled, quartered, cored, sliced thinly

1 Preheat oven to 180°C/350°F. Grease 20cm x 30cm (8-inch x 12-inch) rectangular pan; line base and long sides with baking paper, extending paper 5cm (2 inches) over sides.
2 Make caramel apples.
3 Roll pastry between sheets of baking paper until large enough to line base of pan. Press pastry into pan; trim edges. Refrigerate 20 minutes.
4 Beat butter and sugar in small bowl with electric mixer until light and fluffy; beat in eggs, one at a time. Stir in ground almonds, sifted flour and rind. Spread mixture over pastry in pan; top with caramel apples. Bake about 30 minutes. Cool slice in pan before cutting.
5 Reheat caramel sauce; drizzle over apples before serving.

caramel apples Melt the butter in large frying pan over medium heat; add the sugar and apple. Cook, stirring occasionally, about 5 minutes or until apple is lightly caramelised. Remove from heat; cool 20 minutes. Place apple in medium bowl; reserve caramel sauce in frying pan.

prep + cook time 55 minutes
(+ cooling & refrigeration)
makes 24
Slice is best eaten on the day it is made.

oats & grains

rhubarb crumble squares

90g (3 ounces) butter, softened
1 cup (220g) caster (superfine) sugar
1 egg
⅔ cup (100g) plain (all-purpose) flour
¼ cup (35g) self-raising flour
6 trimmed rhubarb stems (375g),
  chopped coarsely
2 tablespoons water
crumble topping
2 cups (180g) rolled oats
½ cup (110g) firmly packed light brown sugar
100g (3 ounces) butter, melted

1 Preheat oven to 180°C/350°F. Grease 20cm x 30cm (8-inch x 12-inch) rectangular pan; line base and long sides with baking paper, extending paper 5cm (2 inches) over sides.
2 Beat butter, ½ cup (110g) of the sugar and egg in small bowl with electric mixer until light and fluffy; stir in sifted flours. Spread mixture into pan. Bake 15 minutes.
3 Meanwhile, combine rhubarb, remaining sugar and the water in medium saucepan; cook, covered, about 7 minutes or until rhubarb softens. Drain rhubarb; reserve syrup for another use.
4 Meanwhile, make crumble.
5 Increase oven temperature to 200°C/400°F. Remove base from oven; top with drained rhubarb, sprinkle with crumble. Bake about 15 minutes. Cool slice in pan before cutting.

crumble topping Combine ingredients in medium bowl.

prep + cook time 45 minutes
makes 24
tips You can make rhubarb cordial with the syrup if you like. Add water or lemonade, a few ice-cubes and a few crushed raspberries. It's best to use traditional rolled oats in this recipe.
Store squares in an airtight container for up to 3 days.

peanut, plum and oat slice

1½ cups (225g) plain (all-purpose) flour
100g (3 ounces) butter, chopped coarsely
½ cup (110g) caster (superfine) sugar
¼ cup (60ml) cold water
1¼ cups (175g) coarsely chopped roasted
    unsalted peanuts
⅔ cup (60g) rolled oats
60g (2 ounces) butter, melted
½ cup (160g) plum jam

1 Preheat oven to 200°C/400°F. Grease 20cm x 30cm (8-inch x 12-inch) rectangular pan; line base and long sides with baking paper, extending paper 5cm (2 inches) over sides.
2 Process flour, chopped butter and 1 tablespoon of the sugar until crumbly. Add the water; process until ingredients come together. Press dough into pan; bake 15 minutes.
3 Meanwhile, combine peanuts, oats, melted butter and remaining sugar in medium bowl.
4 Spread base with jam; sprinkle with peanut mixture. Bake about 20 minutes. Cool slice in pan before cutting.

prep + cook time 45 minutes
makes 32
Store slice in an airtight container for up to 3 days.

banana slice with muesli topping

1¼ cups (185g) self-raising flour
1 teaspoon ground cinnamon
80g (2½ ounces) butter, chopped coarsely
½ cup (110g) firmly packed light brown sugar
1 egg, beaten lightly
¼ cup (60ml) milk
2 large overripe bananas (460g), mashed
½ cup (55g) untoasted natural muesli

1 Preheat oven to 180°C/350°F. Grease 20cm x 30cm
(8-inch x 12-inch) rectangular pan; line base and
long sides with baking paper, extending paper 5cm
(2 inches) over sides.
2 Sift flour and cinnamon into large bowl; rub in
butter. Stir in sugar, egg, milk and banana; do not
over-mix. Spread mixture into pan; sprinkle with
muesli. Bake about 25 minutes. Cool slice in pan
before cutting.

prep + cook time 40 minutes
makes 16
Store slice in an airtight container for up to a week.

chewy carrot, oat and walnut slice

125g (4 ounces) butter, melted
1 cup (220g) firmly packed light brown sugar
1 egg
1½ cups (135g) rolled oats
¾ cup (75g) coarsely chopped walnuts
1 medium carrot (120g), grated finely
¾ cup (110g) plain (all-purpose) flour
¼ cup (35g) self-raising flour
lemon glaze
1 cup (160g) pure icing (confectioners') sugar
1 egg white
1 tablespoon lemon juice

1 Preheat oven to 180°C/350°F. Grease 20cm x 30cm (8-inch x 12-inch) rectangular pan; line base and long sides with baking paper, extending paper 5cm (2 inches) over sides.
2 Combine butter, sugar, egg, oats, nuts and carrot in medium bowl; stir in sifted flours. Spread mixture into pan; bake about 30 minutes.
3 Meanwhile, make lemon glaze.
4 Drizzle glaze over hot slice; bake about 5 minutes or until glaze forms a crust. Cool slice in pan before cutting.

lemon glaze Sift icing sugar into small bowl; stir in egg white and juice until smooth.

prep + cook time 45 minutes **makes** 24
Store slice in an airtight container for up to 4 days.

cherry squares with coconut ice frosting

125g (4 ounces) butter, chopped coarsely
¼ cup (55g) caster (superfine) sugar
⅓ cup (60ml) light corn syrup
8 cups (320g) corn flakes
½ cup (40g) toasted shredded coconut
1 cup (100g) halved red glacé cherries
coconut ice frosting
1½ cups (240g) pure icing (confectioners') sugar
1 cup (80g) desiccated coconut
1 egg white
2 tablespoons boiling water, approximately
pink food colouring

1 Grease 20cm x 30cm (8-inch x 12-inch) rectangular pan; line base and long sides with baking paper, extending paper 5cm (2 inches) over sides.
2 Stir butter, sugar and syrup in small saucepan over low heat until sugar dissolves; bring to the boil. Reduce heat; simmer, uncovered, without stirring, 5 minutes.
3 Meanwhile, coarsely crush corn flakes with hands in large bowl until approximately half the volume; stir in coconut and cherries.
4 Stir butter mixture into cornflake mixture. Spread mixture into pan; press down firmly. Cover; refrigerate 30 minutes or until firm.
5 Make coconut ice frosting.
6 Spread frosting over slice; cut into squares when firm.

coconut ice frosting Sift icing sugar into medium bowl; stir in coconut and egg white until combined. Add enough of the water until icing is spreadable; tint frosting pink.

prep + cook time 35 minutes (+ refrigeration)
makes 35
Store squares in an airtight container in the fridge for up to a week.

fruit crackle slice

1 cup (140g) seeded dried dates
⅓ cup (75g) caster (superfine) sugar
90g (3 ounces) butter, chopped coarsely
½ teaspoon mixed spice
4 cups (140g) rice bubbles
½ cup (40g) desiccated coconut

1 Grease 20cm x 30cm (8-inch x 12-inch) rectangular pan; line base and long sides with baking paper, extending paper 5cm (2 inches) over sides.
2 Combine dates, sugar and butter in small heavy-based saucepan. Stir over low heat about 15 minutes or until dates become soft and pulpy. Remove from heat; stir in spice.
3 Combine rice bubbles and warm date mixture in large bowl. Press mixture firmly into pan; sprinkle with coconut, press down firmly. Refrigerate about 1 hour or until firm. Stand at room temperature 10 minutes before cutting.

prep + cook time 35 minutes (+ refrigeration)
makes 35
Store slice in an airtight container for up to a week.

choc-coconut crunch

125g (4 ounces) unsalted butter, chopped coarsely
½ cup (110g) firmly packed dark brown sugar
⅓ cup (80ml) light corn syrup
6 cups (270g) coco pops
1 cup (80g) desiccated coconut
75g (2½ ounces) dark eating (semi-sweet)
   chocolate, melted

1 Grease 20cm x 30cm (8-inch x 12-inch) rectangular pan; line base and long sides with baking paper, extending paper 5cm (2 inches) over sides.
2 Combine butter, sugar and corn syrup in medium saucepan; stir over low heat until sugar dissolves.
3 Combine coco pops and coconut in large bowl; stir in butter mixture. Press mixture firmly into pan. Drizzle slice with chocolate; refrigerate 1 hour or until firm. Stand at room temperature 10 minutes before cutting into pieces.

prep + cook time 25 minutes (+ refrigeration)
makes 36
Store crunch in an airtight container for up to a week.

anzac slice with golden icing

125g (4 ounces) unsalted butter, chopped coarsely
1 cup (220g) firmly packed light brown sugar
2 tablespoons golden syrup or treacle
¼ cup (60ml) water
½ teaspoon bicarbonate of soda (baking soda)
½ cup (40g) desiccated coconut
1 cup (90g) rolled oats
1 cup (150g) plain (all-purpose) flour
golden icing
2 cups (320g) icing (confectioners') sugar
1 tablespoon golden syrup or treacle
20g (¾ ounce) unsalted butter
2 tablespoons hot water, approximately

1 Preheat oven to 120°C/250°F. Grease 24cm x 32cm (9½-inch x 13-inch) swiss roll pan; line base and long sides with baking paper, extending paper 5cm (2 inches) over sides.
2 Stir butter, sugar and syrup in medium saucepan over low heat until sugar dissolves. Remove from heat. Stir in the combined water and soda. Stir in coconut, oats and sifted flour. Spread mixture into pan; bake about 45 minutes. Stand slice in pan 15 minutes before transferring to wire rack to cool.
3 Meanwhile, make golden icing.
4 Spread slice with icing; stand at room temperature until set before cutting.

golden icing Sift icing sugar into medium heatproof bowl; stir in syrup, butter and enough of the water to make a thick paste. Set bowl over medium saucepan of simmering water; stir until icing is spreadable.

prep + cook time 1 hour (+ standing)
makes 40
tip If you want the slice to be fudgy in texture decrease the baking time by 5 to 10 minutes.
Store slice in an airtight container for up to a week.

tropical muesli slice

125g (4 ounces) unsalted butter, chopped coarsely
⅓ cup (75g) firmly packed light brown sugar
2 tablespoons honey
1½ cups (135g) rolled oats
½ cup (75g) self-raising flour
1½ cups (225g) finely chopped dried tropical fruit
⅓ cup (25g) desiccated coconut

1 Preheat oven to 160°C/325°F. Grease 20cm x 30cm (8-inch x 12-inch) rectangular pan; line base and long sides with baking paper, extending paper 5cm (2 inches) over sides.
2 Stir butter, sugar and honey in medium saucepan over low heat until sugar dissolves. Stir in remaining ingredients. Press mixture firmly into pan. Bake about 40 minutes.
3 Cool slice in pan before cutting.

prep + cook time 55 minutes
makes 21
note We used dried pineapple, papaya and mango in this recipe.
Store slice in an airtight container for up to a week.

chocolate crackle slice

185g (6 ounces) dark eating (semi-sweet)
   chocolate, chopped coarsely
100g (3½ ounces) unsalted butter,
   chopped coarsely
½ cup (175g) golden syrup or treacle
4 cups (140g) rice bubbles
185g (6 ounces) dark eating (semi-sweet)
   chocolate, melted
2 teaspoons cocoa powder

1 Grease 20cm x 30cm (8-inch x 12-inch) rectangular pan; line base and long sides with baking paper, extending paper 5cm (2 inches) over sides.
2 Stir chopped chocolate and butter in medium saucepan over low heat until smooth. Remove from heat; stir in syrup and rice bubbles.
3 Spread melted chocolate over base of pan; top with rice bubble mixture, press down gently. Refrigerate 2 hours or until firm. Dust slice with sifted cocoa powder before cutting.

prep + cook time 40 minutes (+ refrigeration)
makes 48
Store slice in airtight container in fridge for up to a week.

dried apple and cranberry muesli slice

2 cups (220g) untoasted natural muesli
1 cup (150g) self-raising flour
½ cup (30g) coarsely chopped dried apples
½ cup (65g) dried cranberries
½ cup (110g) caster (superfine) sugar
155g (5 ounces) butter, chopped coarsely
¼ cup (90g) honey
2 eggs, beaten lightly
pink icing
½ cup (80g) icing (confectioners') sugar
1 tablespoon hot water
¼ teaspoon vegetable oil
pink food colouring

1 Preheat oven to 180°C/350°F. Grease 20cm x 30cm (8-inch x 12-inch) rectangular pan; line base and long sides with baking paper, extending paper 5cm (2 inches) over sides.
2 Combine muesli, sifted flour, fruit and sugar in large bowl.
3 Combine butter and honey in small saucepan; stir over low heat until smooth. Stir butter mixture and eggs into muesli mixture until combined. Spread mixture into pan; bake about 25 minutes. Cool slice in pan.
4 Meanwhile, make pink icing. Drizzle icing over slice before cutting.

pink icing Combine sifted icing sugar, the water and oil in small bowl; tint icing pink.

prep + cook time 40 minutes
makes 24
Store slice in an airtight container for up to a week.

crunchy chocolate squares

155g (5 ounces) milk eating chocolate,
  chopped coarsely
125g (4 ounces) butter, chopped coarsely
½ cup (110g) firmly packed light brown sugar
1 egg, beaten lightly
1½ cups (225g) self-raising flour
4 weet-bix (70g), crushed finely
chocolate glaze
1½ cups (240g) pure icing (confectioners') sugar
2 tablespoons cocoa powder
2 tablespoons hot water, approximately

1 Preheat oven to 180°C/350°F. Grease 20cm x 30cm
(8-inch x 12-inch) rectangular pan; line base and
long sides with baking paper, extending paper 5cm
(2 inches) over sides.
2 Stir chocolate and butter in small saucepan over
low heat until smooth. Transfer mixture to large bowl;
cool 10 minutes.
3 Stir in sugar, egg, sifted flour and weet-bix.
Spread mixture into pan; smooth surface. Bake
about 10 minutes. Cool slice in pan.
4 Make chocolate glaze.
5 Spread slice with glaze; stand at room temperature
until set before cutting into pieces.

chocolate glaze Sift icing sugar and cocoa into
small bowl. Add enough of the hot water to make
glaze spreadable.

prep + cook time 30 minutes (+ standing)
makes 20
Store squares in an airtight container for up to 4 days.

honey, walnut and oat squares

1 cup (150g) self-raising flour
1 cup (220g) caster (superfine) sugar
1 cup (90g) rolled oats
1 cup (80g) desiccated coconut
⅔ cup (70g) coarsely chopped walnuts
2 eggs, beaten lightly
125g (4 ounces) unsalted butter, melted, cooled
1 tablespoon creamed honey
½ cup (55g) coarsely chopped walnuts,
   roasted, extra
honey icing
1 cup (160g) icing (confectioners') sugar
45g (1½ ounces) unsalted butter, melted
1 teaspoon creamed honey
1 tablespoon hot water, approximately

1 Preheat oven to 160°C/325°F. Grease 24cm x 32cm (9½-inch x 13-inch) swiss roll pan; line base and long sides with baking paper, extending paper 5cm (2 inches) over sides.
2 Combine sifted flour, sugar, oats, coconut and nuts in large bowl. Stir in eggs, butter and honey. Press mixture firmly into pan. Bake about 25 minutes. Cool slice in pan.
3 Meanwhile, make honey icing.
4 Drizzle slice with honey icing; sprinkle with extra nuts. Let icing set at room temperature before cutting slice.

honey icing Combine sifted icing sugar in small bowl with butter, honey and enough of the hot water to make icing pourable.

prep + cook time 40 minutes
makes 30
Store in an airtight container for up to a week.

chocolate & coffee

mocha hedgehog slice

⅓ cup (50g) raisins
¼ cup (60ml) hot strong coffee
400g (12½ ounces) dark eating (semi-sweet)
   chocolate, chopped coarsely
155g (5 ounces) butter, chopped coarsely
1 egg
¼ cup (55g) caster (superfine) sugar
185g (6 ounces) shortbread biscuits,
   chopped coarsely
1 cup (140g) unsalted macadamias, roasted,
   chopped coarsely

1 Combine raisins and coffee in small bowl;
stand 1 hour.
2 Grease 20cm x 30cm (8-inch x 12-inch) rectangular
pan; line base and long sides with baking paper,
extending paper 5cm (2 inches) over sides.
3 Stir chocolate and butter in medium heatproof
bowl over medium saucepan of simmering water
until smooth.
4 Beat egg and sugar in small bowl with electric
mixer until thick and doubled in volume. Stir into
chocolate mixture. Fold coffee mixture and remaining
ingredients into egg mixture.
5 Spread mixture into pan. Cover surface with
plastic wrap, smooth surface with spatula or hands.
Refrigerate 3 hours or overnight before cutting.

prep + cook time 20 minutes
(+ standing & refrigeration)
makes 40
Store slice in an airtight container in the fridge for up
to a week. Serve straight from the fridge.

wicked choc-mint rocky road

600g (1¼ pounds) dark eating (semi-sweet)
   chocolate, chopped coarsely
250g (8 ounces) white marshmallows
1 cup (140g) unsalted pistachios, roasted,
   chopped coarsely
½ cup (80g) blanched almonds, roasted,
   chopped coarsely
½ cup (40g) shredded coconut, toasted
2 cups (375g) mint leaf lollies

1 Grease 20cm x 30cm (8-inch x 12-inch) rectangular
pan; line base and long sides with baking paper,
extending paper 5cm (2 inches) over sides.
2 Stir chocolate in large heatproof bowl over large
saucepan of simmering water until smooth. Working
quickly, stir in remaining ingredients; spread mixture
into pan. Refrigerate 3 hours or overnight before
cutting into pieces

prep + cook time 15 minutes (+ refrigeration)
makes 60
tip The mint leaves used in this recipe are sometimes
called spearmint leaves – they are a firm leaf-shaped,
mint-flavoured confection.
Store rocky road in an airtight container in the
fridge for up to two weeks. Slice is best served
at room temperature.

choc-malt slice

250g (8 ounces) plain chocolate biscuits
280g (9 ounces) choc-coated malt balls
100g (3 ounces) unsalted butter, chopped coarsely
½ cup (125ml) sweetened condensed milk
400g (12½ ounces) milk eating chocolate,
    chopped coarsely
1 tablespoon vegetable oil

1 Grease 20cm x 30cm (8-inch x 12-inch) rectangular pan; line base and long sides with baking paper, extending paper 5cm (2 inches) over sides.
2 Process 200g (6½ ounces) of the biscuits until fine; chop remaining biscuits coarsely.
3 Reserve 40 whole choc-malt balls; coarsely chop 1 cup of the remaining balls. Reserve any extra choc-malt balls for another use.
4 Stir butter and condensed milk in small saucepan over low heat until smooth.
5 Combine processed and chopped biscuits with chopped choc-malt balls in medium bowl; stir in butter mixture. Press mixture into pan. Refrigerate 30 minutes.
6 Stir chocolate and oil in medium heatproof bowl over medium saucepan of simmering water until smooth; spread over biscuit base. Top with reserved choc-malt balls. Refrigerate about 1 hour or until set before cutting.

prep + cook time 20 minutes (+ refrigeration)
makes 40
tip Use un-iced, unfilled plain biscuits for this recipe.
Store slice in an airtight container in the fridge for up to 4 days.

white chocolate, pineapple and coconut slice

90g (3 ounces) butter, chopped coarsely
250g (8 ounces) white eating chocolate,
  chopped coarsely
440g (14 ounces) canned crushed pineapple in
  natural juice
½ cup (110g) caster (superfine) sugar
2 eggs
1½ cups (225g) plain (all-purpose) flour
½ cup (75g) self-raising flour
½ cup (40g) desiccated coconut
1½ cups (240g) pure icing (confectioners') sugar
⅓ cup (25g) shredded coconut

1 Preheat oven to 160°C/325°F. Grease 24cm x 32cm (9½-inch x 13-inch) swiss roll pan; line base and long sides with baking paper, extending paper 5cm (2 inches) over sides.
2 Stir butter and chocolate in medium saucepan over low heat until smooth. Cool 10 minutes.
3 Meanwhile, drain pineapple well over medium bowl. Reserve 2 tablespoons juice.
4 Stir caster sugar, eggs, sifted flours, desiccated coconut and drained pineapple into chocolate mixture; spread mixture into pan. Bake about 35 minutes. Cool slice in pan before icing.
5 Meanwhile, sift icing sugar into medium heatproof bowl; stir in reserved pineapple juice. Set bowl over medium saucepan of simmering water; stir until icing is spreadable.
6 Spread icing over slice; sprinkle with shredded coconut. Stand at room temperature until icing sets before cutting.

prep + cook time 55 minutes (+ standing)
makes 35
tip Do not overheat or over-stir chocolate mixture or it will "split".
Store slice in an airtight container for up to a week.

hazelnut chocolate squares

185g (6 ounces) butter, softened
1 cup (220g) caster (superfine) sugar
4 eggs
2 cups (200g) ground hazelnuts
¼ cup (35g) plain (all-purpose) flour
300g (9½ ounces) milk eating chocolate,
    chopped coarsely
2 teaspoons vegetable oil

1 Preheat oven to 180°C/350°F. Grease 24cm x 32cm (9½-inch x 13-inch) swiss roll pan; line base and long sides with baking paper, extending paper 5cm (2 inches) over sides.
2 Beat butter and sugar in medium bowl with electric mixer until light and fluffy. Beat in eggs, one at a time; stir in ground hazelnuts and sifted flour. Spread mixture into pan; bake about 20 minutes. Stand slice in pan 15 minutes.
3 Meanwhile, stir chocolate and oil in medium heatproof bowl over medium saucepan of simmering water until smooth; spread chocolate mixture over slice. Refrigerate until set before cutting

prep + cook time 40 minutes
(+ standing & refrigeration)
makes 48
tip To achieve a smooth chocolate glaze, spread the glaze over the slice with a spatula, then tap the pan gently on the bench until the glaze becomes smooth.
Store squares in an airtight container for up to a week.

chocolate liqueur truffle squares

185g (6 ounces) milk eating chocolate, chopped coarsely
2 teaspoons vegetable oil
¾ cup (180ml) thickened (heavy) cream
500g (1 pound) dark eating (semi-sweet) chocolate, chopped finely
¼ cup (60ml) hazelnut-flavoured liqueur
1 cup (140g) roasted hazelnuts, chopped finely

1 Grease 20cm x 30cm (8-inch x 12-inch) rectangular pan; line base and long sides with baking paper, extending paper 5cm (2 inches) over sides.
2 Stir milk chocolate and oil in small heatproof bowl over small saucepan of simmering water until smooth; spread over base of pan. Freeze 5 minutes.
3 Meanwhile, bring cream to the boil in medium saucepan. Remove from heat; add dark chocolate, stir until smooth. Stir in liqueur. Spread over milk chocolate in pan; sprinkle with nuts. Refrigerate 3 hours or overnight before cutting into pieces.

prep + cook time 20 minutes (+ refrigeration)
makes 96
Store squares in an airtight container in the fridge for up to a week.

double chocolate and raspberry brownies

275g (9 ounces) dark eating (semi-sweet) chocolate, chopped coarsely
155g (5 ounces) butter, chopped coarsely
1½ cups (330g) caster (superfine) sugar
3 eggs, beaten lightly
1½ cups (225g) plain (all-purpose) flour
155g (5 ounces) frozen raspberries
155g (5 ounces) white eating chocolate, chopped coarsely

1 Preheat oven to 180°C/350°F. Grease 20cm x 30cm (8-inch x 12-inch) rectangular pan; line base and long sides with baking paper, extending paper 5cm (2 inches) over sides.
2 Stir dark chocolate and butter in large heatproof bowl over large saucepan of simmering water until smooth; stir in sugar. Remove from heat; stir in eggs, then sifted flour, raspberries and white chocolate.
3 Spread mixture into pan; bake about 25 minutes. Cool brownie in pan before cutting.

prep + cook time 40 minutes **makes** 40
tip Use the raspberries while they are still frozen for best results.
Store in an airtight container for up to a week.

choc-raspberry lamington slice

6 eggs
⅔ cup (150g) caster (superfine) sugar
⅓ cup (50g) cornflour (cornstarch)
½ cup (75g) plain (all-purpose) flour
⅓ cup (50g) self-raising flour
1 cup (250ml) thickened (heavy) cream
½ cup (160g) raspberry jam
1 cup (80g) desiccated coconut
chocolate icing
4½ cups (720g) icing (confectioners') sugar
½ cup (50g) cocoa powder
15g (½ ounce) butter, melted
½ cup (125ml) milk, approximately

1 Preheat oven to 180°C/350°F. Grease two 24cm x 32cm (9½-inch x 13-inch) swiss roll pans; line bases and long sides with baking paper, extending paper 5cm (2 inches) over sides.
2 To make sponges, beat eggs in medium bowl with electric mixer about 10 minutes or until thick and creamy; gradually add sugar, beating until dissolved. Fold in triple-sifted flours.
3 Divide and spread sponge mixture between pans. Bake about 15 minutes. Turn cakes immediately onto baking-paper-covered wire racks to cool.
4 Beat cream in small bowl with electric mixer until firm peaks form.
5 Spread one cake with jam, then with cream to within 1cm of the edge of the sponge. Top with remaining cake; place on wire rack.
6 Make chocolate icing; spread icing all over top and sides of slice. Sprinkle top and sides with coconut; refrigerate until set before cutting.

chocolate icing Sift icing sugar and cocoa into medium heatproof bowl; stir in butter and enough milk to make a thick paste. Set bowl over medium saucepan of simmering water; stir until icing is spreadable.

prep + cook time 45 minutes (+ refrigeration)
makes 30
tip Leaving a 1cm border of sponge without cream will make the icing of the sides of the slice easier to do. The weight of the top layer of sponge will push the cream far enough.
Store slice in an airtight container in the fridge for up to 3 days.

coffee and hazelnut oat slice

125g (4 ounces) butter, chopped coarsely
1 cup (220g) firmly packed light brown sugar
1 tablespoon instant coffee granules
1¼ cups (110g) rolled oats
¾ cup (75g) coarsely chopped roasted hazelnuts
1 egg
¾ cup (110g) plain (all-purpose) flour
¼ cup (35g) self-raising flour
½ teaspoon bicarbonate of soda (baking soda)
½ cup (95g) dark choc bits
185g (6 ounces) dark eating (semi-sweet)
   chocolate, melted

1 Preheat oven to 160°C/325°F. Grease 20cm x 30cm (8-inch x 12-inch) rectangular pan; line base and long sides with baking paper, extending paper 5cm (2 inches) over sides.
2 Melt butter in medium saucepan. Remove from heat; stir in sugar and coffee until smooth.
3 Stir oats and nuts into butter mixture, then egg, sifted dry ingredients and choc bits.
4 Spread mixture into pan; bake about 25 minutes. Cover hot slice with foil; cool.
5 Spread melted chocolate over slice; stand at room temperature until set before cutting.

prep + cook time 45 minutes (+ cooling & standing)
makes 30
Store slice in airtight container for up to a week.

peanut butter and jam brownie

155g (5 ounces) unsalted butter, chopped coarsely
360g (11½ ounces) dark eating (semi-sweet)
  chocolate, chopped coarsely
1½ cups (330g) firmly packed light brown sugar
3 eggs
¾ cup (110g) plain (all-purpose) flour
½ cup (120g) sour cream
½ cup (120g) raspberry jam, warmed, strained
peanut butter filling
⅓ cup (95g) smooth peanut butter
45g (1½ ounces) unsalted butter, melted
¼ cup (40g) icing (confectioners') sugar

1 Preheat oven to 160°C/325°F. Grease 24cm x 32cm (9½-inch x 13-inch) swiss roll pan; line base and long sides with baking paper, extending paper 5cm (2 inches) over sides.
2 Make peanut butter filling.
3 Stir butter and chocolate in medium saucepan over low heat until smooth. Remove from heat; stir in sugar, then eggs, sifted flour and sour cream. Spread mixture into pan.
4 Drop alternate rounded teaspoons of peanut butter filling and jam onto brownie mixture; swirl together using a skewer.
5 Bake about 40 minutes. Cool brownie in pan before cutting.

peanut butter filling Combine all ingredients in small bowl.

prep + cook time 55 minutes
makes 24
Store brownies in airtight container for up to a week.

cappuccino mousse squares

250g (8 ounces) plain chocolate biscuits
155g (5 ounces) unsalted butter, melted
1 cup (250ml) thickened (heavy) cream, whipped
2 teaspoons cocoa powder
cappuccino mousse filling
185g (6 ounces) dark eating (semi-sweet)
    chocolate, melted
1 egg, separated
2 teaspoons instant coffee granules
⅓ cup (80ml) thickened (heavy) cream, whipped
¼ cup (55g) caster (superfine) sugar

1 Grease 20cm x 30cm (8-inch x 12-inch) rectangular pan; line base and long sides with baking paper, extending paper 5cm (2 inches) over sides.
2 Process biscuits until fine. Add butter; process until combined. Press mixture over base of pan. Refrigerate 30 minutes.
3 Meanwhile, make cuppuccino mousse filling.
4 Spread filling over biscuit base in pan. Cover; refrigerate 3 hours or overnight until set.
5 Spread whipped cream over mousse filling; dust with sifted cocoa powder.

cappuccino mousse filling Combine melted chocolate, egg yolk and coffee in medium bowl; fold in cream. Beat egg white and sugar in small bowl with electric mixer until thick and sugar dissolved. Fold into chocolate mixture, in two batches.

prep + cook time 25 minutes (+ refrigeration)
makes 24
tip Use un-iced, unfilled plain biscuits for this recipe.
Store squares in an airtight container in the fridge for up to 4 days.

best-ever fudge brownies

185g (6 ounces) unsalted butter, chopped coarsely
300g (10½ ounces) dark eating (semi-sweet)
   chocolate, chopped coarsely
¼ cup (25g) cocoa powder
1 cup (220g) firmly packed light brown sugar
¾ cup (165g) caster (superfine) sugar
2 teaspoons vanilla extract
4 eggs
1½ cups (225g) plain (all-purpose) flour
2 teaspoons cocoa powder, extra

1 Preheat oven to 170°C/340°F. Grease 20cm x 30cm
(8-inch x 12-inch) rectangular pan; line base and
long sides with baking paper, extending paper 5cm
(2 inches) over sides.
2 Stir butter and chocolate in medium saucepan
over low heat until smooth. Remove from heat; whisk
in sifted cocoa, sugars and extract until smooth.
3 Stir eggs and sifted flour into chocolate mixture.
Pour mixture into pan; spread evenly.
4 Bake about 40 minutes. Cool brownie in pan.
Dust with extra sifted cocoa before cutting.

prep + cook time 1 hour
makes 96
tip The mixture should be barely warm when the
eggs and flour are added. Use a bamboo skewer
to test if the brownie is cooked, the skewer should
feel moist, if you want a fudgy brownie; if not, bake
the brownie another 5 minutes or so.
Store in an airtight container in the fridge for up to a
week. They are best served at room temperature.

white chocolate and raspberry rocky road

200g (6½ ounces) shortbread biscuits,
   chopped finely
¾ cup (150g) raspberry lollies, quartered
60g (2 ounces) mini marshmallows
1 cup (75g) shredded coconut
625g (1¼ pounds) white eating chocolate, melted

1 Grease 20cm x 30cm (8-inch x 12-inch) rectangular
pan; line base and long sides with baking paper,
extending paper 5cm (2 inches) over sides.
2 Combine biscuits, lollies, marshmallows and ¾ cup
(60g) of the coconut in large bowl; stir in chocolate.
Spread mixture into pan; smooth surface. Sprinkle
with remaining coconut.
3 Refrigerate 2 hours or until firm before cutting.

prep + cook time 15 minutes (+ refrigeration)
makes 96
Store rocky road in an airtight container in the fridge
for up to a week.

coffee pecan slice

125g (4 ounces) butter, softened
¼ cup (55g) caster (superfine) sugar
1 cup (150g) plain (all-purpose) flour
¼ cup (35g) self-raising flour
2 cups (280g) pecans, roasted
coffee topping
2 teaspoons instant coffee granules
3 teaspoons boiling water
2 eggs
½ cup (175g) golden syrup or treacle
⅓ cup (75g) firmly packed light brown sugar
60g (2 ounces) butter, melted
2 tablespoons plain (all-purpose) flour

1 Preheat oven to 200°C/400°F. Grease 20cm x 30cm (8-inch x 12-inch) rectangular pan; line base and long sides with baking paper, extending paper 5cm (2 inches) over sides.
2 Beat butter and sugar in small bowl with electric mixer until light and fluffy. Stir in sifted flours, in two batches. Press dough over base of pan. Bake 10 minutes. Cool 10 minutes. Reduce oven temperature to 180°C/350°F.
3 Meanwhile, make the coffee topping.
4 Pour topping over base; top with single layer of nuts. Bake about 25 minutes or until set. Cool slice in pan before cutting.

coffee topping Dissolve coffee in the boiling water in medium heatproof bowl. Whisk in eggs, syrup, sugar, butter and flour until combined.

prep + cook time 1 hour
makes 24
Store slice in an airtight container for up to a week.

mocha mousse slice

125g (4 ounces) butter, chopped coarsely
155g (5 ounces) dark eating (semi-sweet)
   chocolate, chopped coarsely
1 egg
⅓ cup (150g) caster (superfine) sugar
¾ cup (110g) plain (all-purpose) flour
½ cup (75g) self-raising flour
2 teaspoons cocoa powder
mocha mousse
2 teaspoons instant coffee granules
3 teaspoons boiling water
1 cup (250ml) thickened (heavy) cream
155g (5 ounces) milk eating chocolate, melted

1 Preheat oven to 180°C/350°F. Grease 20cm x 30cm (8-inch x 12-inch) rectangular pan; line base and long sides with baking paper, extending paper 5cm (2 inches) over sides.
2 Stir butter and chocolate in medium saucepan over low heat until smooth; cool 10 minutes.
3 Stir egg and sugar into chocolate mixture; stir in sifted flours. Spread mixture into pan. Bake about 15 minutes. Cool base in pan.
4 Meanwhile, make mocha mousse. Pour mousse over base; refrigerate 3 hours or until set.
5 Dust slice with sifted cocoa before cutting.

mocha mousse Dissolve coffee in the boiling water in cup; cool. Beat cream and coffee mixture in small bowl with electric mixer until soft peaks form. Fold in cooled chocolate.

prep + cook time 35 minutes (+ refrigeration)
makes 48
Store slice in an airtight container in the fridge for up to 4 days.

custard & cheesecake

blueberry passionfruit cheesecake squares

250g (8 ounces) plain sweet biscuits
100g (3 ounces) butter, melted
500g (1 pound) cream cheese, softened
¾ cup (165g) caster (superfine) sugar
2 teaspoons finely grated lime rind
2 eggs
½ cup (120g) sour cream
2 tablespoons lime juice
1 cup (150g) frozen blueberries
¼ cup (60ml) passionfruit pulp

1 Preheat oven to 150°C/300°F. Grease 20cm x 30cm (8-inch x 12-inch) rectangular pan; line base and long sides with baking paper, extending paper 5cm (2 inches) over sides.
2 Process biscuits until fine. Add butter; process until combined. Press mixture over base of pan; refrigerate 30 minutes.
3 Beat cream cheese, sugar and rind in medium bowl with electric mixer until smooth. Beat in eggs, one at a time, then sour cream and juice.
4 Pour mixture into pan; sprinkle with blueberries, drizzle with passionfruit pulp. Bake about 35 minutes or until set. Cool in oven with door ajar. Refrigerate 3 hours or overnight before cutting into squares.

prep + cook time 50 minutes
(+ refrigeration & cooling)
makes 15
tips We used granita biscuits for this recipe. Canned or fresh passionfruit pulp can be used.
Store squares in an airtight container in the fridge for up to 2 days.

coffee slice with chocolate glaze

3 cups (750ml) milk
¾ cup (65g) roasted coffee beans
8 egg yolks
¾ cup (165g) caster (superfine) sugar
½ cup (75g) cornflour (cornstarch)
75g (2½ ounces) butter, chopped coarsely
3 sheets puff pastry
chocolate glaze
155g (5 ounces) dark eating (semi-sweet)
   chocolate, chopped coarsely
30g (1 ounce) butter

1 Grease 20cm x 30cm (8-inch x 12-inch) rectangular pan; line base and long sides with baking paper, extending paper 5cm (2 inches) over sides.
2 Bring milk and beans to the boil in medium saucepan, remove from heat; stand 45 minutes.
3 Whisk egg yolks, sugar and cornflour in large bowl until combined. Bring milk mixture back to the boil; whisk into egg mixture. Strain into same pan; discard coffee beans.
4 Whisk custard over high heat until mixture boils and thickens. Remove from heat; whisk in butter. Cover surface of custard with plastic wrap; refrigerate until firm.
5 Meanwhile, preheat oven to 240°C/450°F.
6 Place pastry sheets on separate greased oven trays. Bake about 10 minutes or until puffed and browned lightly; cool. Flatten pastry with hand. Trim 1½ pieces of the pastry to fit base of pan; position in pan puffed-side up.
7 Spread custard over pastry in pan. Trim remaining pastry to fit; position on top of custard puffed-side down, press down gently.
8 Make chocolate glaze; pour over pastry, refrigerate until set before cutting.

chocolate glaze Combine ingredients in small saucepan; stir over low heat until smooth.

prep + cook time 50 minutes
(+ standing & refrigeration)
makes 12
tip You can make the coffee custard the day before. Beat custard with an electric mixer to soften before assembling slice.
Store slice in the fridge; slice is best eaten on the day it is made.

cookies and cream cheesecake slice

300g (9½ ounces) round cream-filled
   chocolate biscuits
1½ teaspoons gelatine
2 tablespoons water
250g (8 ounces) cream cheese, softened
¾ cup (180ml) thickened (heavy) cream
1 teaspoon vanilla extract
⅓ cup (75g) caster (superfine) sugar
125g (4 ounces) white eating chocolate, melted
185g (6 ounces) dark eating (semi-sweet)
   chocolate, chopped coarsely
75g (2½ ounces) unsalted butter, chopped coarsely

1 Grease 20cm x 30cm (8-inch x 12-inch) rectangular
pan; line base and long sides with baking paper,
extending paper 5cm (2 inches) over sides.
2 Place biscuits over base of pan.
3 Sprinkle gelatine over the water in small heatproof
jug. Stand jug in small saucepan of simmering water;
stir until gelatine dissolves. Cool 5 minutes.
4 Beat cream cheese, cream, extract and sugar
in small bowl with electric mixer until smooth. Stir
in gelatine mixture and white chocolate. Pour
cheesecake mixture over biscuits; refrigerate 2 hours.
5 Stir dark chocolate and butter in small saucepan
over low heat until smooth; spread evenly over
cheesecake. Refrigerate overnight before cutting.

prep + cook time 50 minutes (+ refrigeration)
makes 48
Store slice in an airtight container in the fridge for up
to 2 days.

mint-chocolate cheesecake slice

250g (8 ounces) plain chocolate biscuits
120g (4 ounces) butter, melted
3 teaspoons gelatine
2 tablespoons water
500g (1 pound) cream cheese, softened
½ cup (110g) caster (superfine) sugar
1½ cups (375ml) thickened (heavy) cream
¼ cup (60ml) mint-flavoured liqueur
chocolate glaze
185g (6 ounces) dark eating (semi-sweet)
   chocolate, chopped coarsely
50g (1½ ounces) butter

1 Grease 20cm x 30cm (8-inch x 12-inch) rectangular pan; line base and long sides with baking paper, extending paper 5cm (2 inches) over sides.
2 Process biscuits until fine. Add butter; process until combined. Press mixture over base of pan; refrigerate 30 minutes.
3 Meanwhile, sprinkle gelatine over the water in small heatproof jug; stand jug in small saucepan of simmering water. Stir until gelatine dissolves. Cool 5 minutes.
4 Beat cream cheese and sugar in medium bowl with electric mixer until smooth; beat in cream until smooth and thickened slightly. Stir in gelatine mixture and liqueur. Pour filling into pan; refrigerate overnight or until set.
5 Make chocolate glaze; pour over slice, refrigerate until set before cutting.

chocolate glaze Combine ingredients in small saucepan; stir over low heat until smooth.

prep + cook time 30 minutes (+ refrigeration)
makes 20
tip Use un-iced, unfilled plain biscuits for this recipe.
Store slice in an airtight container in the fridge for up to a week.

ginger lime slice

¾ cup (110g) plain (all-purpose) flour
¼ cup (55g) self-raising flour
½ teaspoon bicarbonate of soda (baking soda)
1 teaspoon each ground ginger and mixed spice
¼ cup (55g) firmly packed light brown sugar
65g (2 ounces) butter, chopped coarsely
½ cup (175g) golden syrup or treacle
1 egg, beaten lightly
½ cup (125ml) milk
lime filling
1 teaspoon gelatine
2 tablespoons lime juice
250g (8 ounces) cream cheese, softened
¼ cup (55g) caster (superfine) sugar
2 teaspoons finely grated lime rind
1 cup (250ml) pouring cream

1 Preheat oven to 180°C/350°F. Grease two 24cm x 32cm (9½-inch x 13-inch) swiss roll pans; line bases and long sides with baking paper, extending paper 5cm (2 inches) over sides.
2 To make ginger cake, sift flours, soda and spices into large bowl; stir in brown sugar. Combine butter and syrup in small saucepan; stir over low heat until smooth. Stir butter mixture into flour mixture with egg and milk. Divide mixture between pans; bake about 10 minutes. Cool in pans.
3 Meanwhile, make lime filling.
4 Pour filling over one of the ginger cakes in pan; top with remaining ginger cake. Refrigerate 3 hours or overnight until firm before cutting.

lime filling Sprinkle gelatine over juice in small heatproof jug; stand jug in small saucepan of simmering water. Stir until gelatine dissolves. Cool 5 minutes. Beat cream cheese, sugar and rind in medium bowl with electric mixer until smooth; beat in cream. Stir in gelatine mixture.

prep + cook time 40 minutes (+ refrigeration)
makes 32
Store slice in an airtight container in the fridge for up to a week.

strawberry custard slice

⅔ cup (160ml) milk
½ cup (125ml) pouring cream
1 vanilla bean
4 egg yolks
¼ cup (55g) caster (superfine) sugar
2 tablespoons cornflour (cornstarch)
1¼ cups (185g) plain (all-purpose) flour
¼ cup (40g) icing (confectioners') sugar
125g (4 ounces) unsalted butter, chopped coarsely
2 teaspoons iced water, approximately
250g (8 ounces) strawberries, sliced thinly
2 tablespoons raspberry jam, warmed, strained

1 Grease 20cm x 30cm (8-inch x 12-inch) rectangular pan; line base and long sides with baking paper, extending paper 5cm (2 inches) over sides.
2 Combine milk and cream in medium saucepan. Split vanilla bean; scrape seeds into cream mixture, add bean. Bring cream mixture to the boil. Whisk 3 of the egg yolks, caster sugar and cornflour in small bowl until combined. Discard vanilla bean from cream mixture; gradually whisk hot cream mixture into egg mixture. Return to pan; cook, whisking, until custard mixture boils and thickens. Cool.
3 Meanwhile, blend or process flour, icing sugar and butter until crumbly. Add remaining egg yolk and enough of the water to make ingredients cling together. Knead dough on floured surface until smooth. Press dough over base of pan; prick all over with a fork. Cover with plastic wrap; refrigerate 30 minutes.
4 Preheat oven to 200°C/400°F.
5 Bake base about 15 minutes or until browned lightly; cool.
6 Spread custard over base; top with berries. Brush slice with jam; refrigerate 1 hour before cutting.

prep + cook time 40 minutes (+ refrigeration)
makes 15
Slice is best eaten within 24 hours.

caramel cheesecake slice

200g (6½ ounces) plain sweet biscuits
½ cup (60g) pecans, roasted
100g (3½ ounces) unsalted butter, melted
380g (12 ounces) canned caramel top'n'fill
cheesecake filling
500g (1 pound) cream cheese, softened
2 teaspoons vanilla extract
½ cup (110g) caster (superfine) sugar
2 eggs
1 cup (250ml) thickened (heavy) cream

1 Grease 20cm x 30cm (8-inch x 12-inch) rectangular pan; line base and long sides with baking paper, extending paper 5cm (2 inches) over sides.
2 Process biscuits and nuts until fine. Add butter; process until combined. Press mixture evenly over base of pan. Refrigerate 30 minutes.
3 Preheat oven to140°C/280°F.
4 Make cheesecake filling.
5 Spread caramel over biscuit base; pour cheesecake filling over caramel. Bake about 45 minutes. Cool cheesecake in oven with door ajar. Refrigerate 3 hours or overnight before cutting.

cheesecake filling Beat cream cheese, extract, sugar and eggs in medium bowl with electric mixer until smooth. Gradually beat in cream.

prep + cook time 1 hour (+ cooling & refrigeration)
makes 48
tip We used digestive biscuits in this recipe.
Store slice in an airtight container in the fridge for up

coconut lime squares

250g (8 ounces) plain sweet biscuits
¼ cup (20g) desiccated coconut
125g (4 ounces) unsalted butter, melted
4 eggs
1 cup (220g) caster (superfine) sugar
⅓ cup (50g) plain (all-purpose) flour
1 tablespoon finely grated lime rind
⅔ cup (160ml) lime juice
½ cup (25g) desiccated coconut, extra

1 Grease 20cm x 30cm (8-inch x 12-inch) rectangular pan; line base and long sides with baking paper, extending paper 5cm (2 inches) over sides.
2 Process biscuits and coconut until fine. Add butter; process until combined. Press mixture evenly over base of pan. Refrigerate 30 minutes.
3 Preheat oven to 160°C/325°F.
4 Whisk eggs and sugar in medium bowl until combined. Whisk in sifted flour, rind and juice; pour mixture over base. Bake about 20 minutes. Sprinkle with extra coconut; press down gently. Cool. Refrigerate 3 hours or overnight before cutting.

prep + cook time 35 minutes
(+ cooling & refrigeration)
makes 48
Store squares in an airtight container in the fridge for up to 2 days.

chocolate honeycomb ice-cream slice

1.5 litres (6 cups) vanilla
  ice-cream, softened slightly
½ cup (65g) finely chopped unsalted
  pistachios, roasted
150g (4½ ounces) chocolate-coated honeycomb
  bars, chopped finely
125g (4 ounces) unsalted butter, softened
⅓ cup (55g) caster (superfine) sugar
⅓ cup (55g) firmly packed light brown sugar
½ teaspoon vanilla extract
1 egg
¾ cup (110g) plain (all-purpose) flour
¾ cup (110g) self-raising flour
¼ cup (25g) cocoa powder

1 Line 20cm x 30cm (8-inch x 12-inch) rectangular pan with four layers of plastic wrap, extending plastic wrap 10cm (4 inches) over sides of pan.
2 Place ice-cream in large bowl; fold in nuts and chocolate-coated honeycomb. Working quickly, spoon ice-cream into pan, pressing down firmly and smoothing surface. Fold plastic wrap over to enclose. Freeze 3 hours or overnight until firm.
3 Preheat oven to 170°C/340°F. Remove ice-cream from pan, still wrapped in plastic; place on tray. Return to freezer.
4 Grease two 20cm x 30cm (8-inch x 12-inch) rectangular pans; line bases and long sides with baking paper, extending paper 5cm (2 inches) over sides.
5 To make cookie dough, beat butter, sugars and extract in small bowl with electric mixer until light and fluffy; beat in egg. Transfer mixture to large bowl; stir in sifted flours and cocoa.
6 Divide dough in half; press into pans. Bake about 10 minutes. Stand cookie slices in pans 20 minutes before turning, top-side up, onto wire racks to cool.
7 Place one cookie slice on board; top with ice-cream then remaining cookie slice. Cut into squares; serve immediately.

prep + cook time 1 hour (+ freezing & standing)
makes 15
note If you are not serving the slice immediately, return to the freezer until required. Stand at room temperature for about 5 minutes before cutting.

tiramisu cheesecake squares

2 eggs
⅓ cup (75g) caster (superfine) sugar
½ cup (75g) plain (all-purpose) flour
2 teaspoons instant coffee granules
1 tablespoon boiling water
2 tablespoons marsala
2 teaspoons cocoa powder
cream cheese filling
2 teaspoons gelatine
1 tablespoon boiling water
125g (4 ounces) cream cheese, softened
¼ cup (40g) icing (confectioners') sugar
1 cup (250ml) thickened (heavy) cream
2 tablespoons marsala
250g (8 ounces) mascarpone cheese

1 Preheat oven to 200°C/400°F. Grease 20cm x 30cm (8-inch x 12-inch) rectangular pan; line base and long sides with baking paper, extending paper 5cm (2 inches) over sides.
2 To make sponge, beat eggs and sugar in small bowl with electric mixer until thick and sugar is dissolved. Fold in triple-sifted flour. Spread mixture into pan. Bake about 12 minutes. Cool in pan.
3 Combine coffee, the water and marsala in small bowl. Brush coffee mixture over sponge.
4 Make cream cheese filling.
5 Pour filling over sponge. Refrigerate 3 hours or overnight until set. Dust with sifted cocoa before cutting.

cream cheese filling Sprinkle gelatine over the water in small heatproof jug; stand in small saucepan of simmering water. Stir until gelatine dissolves. Cool 5 minutes. Beat cream cheese and sifted icing sugar in medium bowl with electric mixer until smooth. Add cream and marsala; beat until combined. Stir in mascarpone and gelatine mixture.

prep + cook time 35 minutes (+ refrigeration)
makes 15
Store squares in an airtight container in the fridge for up to 4 days.

white chocolate and berry cheesecake slice

250g (8 ounces) plain sweet biscuits
125g (4 ounces) unsalted butter, melted
3 eggs
¾ cup (165g) caster (superfine) sugar
500g (1 pound) cream cheese, softened
155g (5 ounces) white eating chocolate, melted
2 tablespoons honey
1½ cups (225g) frozen blackberries
1 tablespoon cornflour (cornstarch)

1 Grease 20cm x 30cm (8-inch x 12-inch) rectangular pan; line base and long sides with baking paper, extending paper 5cm (2 inches) over sides.
2 Process biscuits until fine. Add butter; process until combined. Press mixture evenly over base of pan. Refrigerate 30 minutes.
3 Preheat oven to 140°C/280°F.
4 Beat eggs and sugar in small bowl with electric mixer until thick and creamy.
5 Beat cream cheese in medium bowl with electric mixer until smooth; gradually beat in egg mixture. Beat in melted chocolate and honey.
6 Toss frozen berries in cornflour; discard any excess cornflour. Place blackberries evenly on base in pan; pour cream cheese mixture over blackberries, spread evenly. Bake about 30 minutes.
7 Cool cheesecake in oven with door ajar. Refrigerate 3 hours or overnight before cutting.

prep + cook time 50 minutes
(+ cooling & refrigeration)
makes 32
tip Use any type of frozen berry, or a combination of berries. Store slice in an airtight container in the fridge for up to 2 days.

lemon cheesecake squares

250g (8 ounces) butternut snap biscuits
½ cup (40g) flaked almonds
125g (4 ounces) butter, melted
250g (8 ounces) cream cheese, softened
3 teaspoons finely grated lemon rind
395g (12½ ounces) canned sweetened
   condensed milk
⅓ cup (80ml) lemon juice

1 Grease 20cm x 30cm (8-inch x 12-inch) rectangular pan; line base and long sides with baking paper, extending paper 5cm (2 inches) over sides.
2 Process biscuits and nuts until fine. Add butter; process until combined. Press mixture over base of pan. Refrigerate 30 minutes.
3 Beat cream cheese and rind in medium bowl with electric mixer until smooth. Add condensed milk and juice; beat until smooth. Pour cream cheese mixture over base. Refrigerate overnight before cutting.

prep + cook time 20 minutes (+ refrigeration)
makes 24
Store squares in an airtight container in the fridge for up to 4 days.

honey and spice slice

250g (8 ounces) gingernut biscuits
100g (3½ ounces) butter, melted
500g (1 pound) cream cheese, softened
¼ cup (55g) caster (superfine) sugar
¼ cup (90g) honey
1 teaspoon vanilla extract
2 teaspoons mixed spice
½ cup (125ml) pouring cream
2 eggs, separated
2 teaspoons cinnamon sugar

1 Grease 20cm x 30cm (8-inch x 12-inch) rectangular pan; line base and long sides with baking paper, extending paper 5cm (2 inches) over sides.
2 Process biscuits until fine. Add butter; process until combined. Press mixture over base of pan; refrigerate 30 minutes.
3 Preheat oven to 160°C/325°F.
4 Beat cream cheese, sugar, honey, extract and spice in medium bowl with electric mixer until smooth; beat in cream and egg yolks.
5 Beat egg whites in small bowl with electric mixer until soft peaks form; fold into cream cheese mixture.
6 Pour cream cheese mixture into pan; bake about 30 minutes. Cool in oven with door ajar. Refrigerate 3 hours over overnight. Sprinkle with cinnamon sugar before cutting.

prep + cook time 1 hour (+ refrigeration & cooling)
makes 20
Store slice in an airtight container in the fridge for up to 4 days.

fruit & nut

raspberry walnut slice

150g (4½ ounces) butter, softened
⅔ cup (110g) icing (confectioners') sugar
1¾ cups (260g) plain (all-purpose) flour
½ teaspoon ground cinnamon
½ cup (60g) ground walnuts
300g (9½ ounces) frozen raspberries

1 Preheat oven to 180°C/350°F. Grease 20cm x 30cm (8-inch x 12-inch) rectangular pan; line base and long sides with baking paper, extending paper 5cm (2 inches) over sides.
2 Beat butter and sifted icing sugar in medium bowl with electric mixer until light and fluffy. Stir in sifted flour, cinnamon and nuts until mixture is crumbly.
3 Reserve 1 cup of crumble mixture. Press remaining mixture into pan; top with raspberries. Sprinkle with reserved crumble mixture; bake about 40 minutes. Cool slice in pan before cutting.

prep + cook time 55 minutes **makes** 20
tip Walnut halves or pieces can be ground finely in a blender or processor.
Store slice in an airtight container for up to 3 days.

coconut slice with lemon syrup

155g (5 ounces) butter, softened
¾ cup (165g) caster (superfine) sugar
2 teaspoons finely grated lemon rind
2 eggs
1¼ cups (100g) desiccated coconut
1 cup (150g) self-raising flour
2 tablespoons lemon juice
lemon syrup
¼ cup (55g) caster (superfine) sugar
1 tablespoon finely grated lemon rind
⅓ cup (80ml) lemon juice
¼ cup (60ml) water

1 Preheat oven to 180°C/350°F. Grease 20cm x 30cm (8-inch x 12-inch) rectangular pan; line base and long sides with baking paper, extending paper 5cm (2 inches) over sides.
2 Beat butter, sugar and rind in small bowl with electric mixer until light and fluffy; beat in eggs until combined. Transfer mixture to medium bowl; stir in coconut, sifted flour and juice. Spread mixture into pan. Bake about 20 minutes.
3 Meanwhile, make lemon syrup.
4 Pour syrup over hot slice. Cool slice in pan before cutting.

lemon syrup Stir ingredients in small saucepan over low heat until sugar dissolves. Bring to the boil. Reduce heat; simmer, uncovered, about 10 minutes or until syrup thickens slightly.

prep + cook time 35 minutes
makes 25
tip You'll need 3 lemons to make this recipe.
Store slice in an airtight container for up to a week.

apple-cinnamon custard squares

100g (3 ounces) butter, softened
¼ cup (55g) caster (superfine) sugar
1 egg
⅔ cup (100g) self-raising flour
2 tablespoons custard powder
2 large apples (400g), quartered, cored,
   sliced thinly
20g (¾ ounce) butter, melted
2 teaspoons caster (superfine) sugar, extra
½ teaspoon ground cinnamon

custard

1 tablespoon custard powder
2 tablespoons caster (superfine) sugar
½ cup (125ml) milk
10g (⅓ ounces) butter
1 teaspoon vanilla extract

1 Make custard.
2 Preheat oven to 180°C/350°F. Grease 20cm x 30cm (8-inch x 12-inch) rectangular pan; line base and long sides with baking paper, extending paper 5cm (2 inches) over sides.
3 Beat softened butter and sugar in small bowl with electric mixer until light and fluffy. Beat in egg until combined. Stir in sifted flour and custard powder.
4 Spread mixture into pan; top with custard. Arrange apple on custard; brush with melted butter. Sprinkle with combined extra sugar and cinnamon.
5 Bake about 35 minutes; cool slice in pan before cutting. Serve warm or at room temperature.

custard Combine custard powder and sugar in small saucepan; gradually blend in milk. Stir over heat until mixture boils and thickens slightly. Remove from heat; stir in butter and extract. Press plastic wrap over surface of custard to prevent a skin forming; cool. Whisk until smooth just before using.

prep + cook time 50 minutes **makes** 15
tip We used unpeeled red-skinned apples for this recipe.
Store squares in an airtight container in the fridge for up to 3 days.

frangipane cherry squares

170g (5½ ounces) butter, softened
¾ cup (165g) caster (superfine) sugar
3 eggs
1 cup (120g) ground almonds
⅓ cup (50g) plain (all-purpose) flour
300g (9½ ounces) frozen cherries
¼ cup (20g) flaked almonds
2 teaspoons icing (confectioners') sugar

1 Preheat oven to 180°C/350°F. Grease 20cm x 30cm (8-inch x 12-inch) rectangular pan; line base and long sides with baking paper, extending paper 5cm (2 inches) over sides.
2 Beat butter and sugar in medium bowl with electric mixer until light and fluffy; beat in eggs until combined. Stir in ground almonds and sifted flour; spread mixture into pan. Top with cherries, pressing down gently; sprinkle with flaked almonds. Bake about 30 minutes. Cool slice in pan.
3 Dust slice with sifted icing sugar before cutting. Serve warm or at room temperature.

prep + cook time 40 minutes **makes** 24
Store squares in an airtight container for up to 4 days.

lemony coconut squares

125g (4 ounces) butter, melted
1 cup (220g) caster (superfine) sugar
1 egg
2 teaspoons finely grated lemon rind
½ cup (75g) plain (all-purpose) flour
¼ cup (35g) self-raising flour
¾ cup (60g) desiccated coconut
10 yellow ready-made sugar flowers
10 white ready-made sugar flowers
lemon glacé icing
2 cups (320g) pure icing (confectioners') sugar
2 tablespoons lemon juice, approximately

1 Preheat oven to 180°C/350°F. Grease 20cm x 30cm (8-inch x 12-inch) rectangular pan; line base and long sides with baking paper, extending paper 5cm (2 inches) over sides.
2 Combine butter, sugar, egg and rind in medium bowl; stir in sifted flours then ½ cup (40g) of the coconut. Spread mixture into pan; bake about 30 minutes. Cool slice in pan.
3 Make lemon glacé icing.
4 Working quickly, spread slice with icing; sprinkle with remaining coconut. Decorate slice with sugar flowers, pressing firmly into icing. Stand slice at room temperature until icing sets before cutting.

lemon glacé icing Sift icing sugar into medium heatproof bowl; stir in enough of the juice to make a thick paste. Set bowl over medium saucepan of simmering water; stir icing until spreadable.

prep + cook time 45 minutes (+ standing)
makes 20
tip Sugar flowers of many shapes, sizes and colours can be bought from most supermarkets and cake decorating shops.
Store squares in an airtight container for up to 4 days.

fruit mince squares

155g (5 ounces) butter, softened
⅔ cup (150g) caster (superfine) sugar
2 eggs
1 cup (150g) self-raising flour
½ cup (75g) plain (all-purpose) flour
½ cup (125ml) milk
¾ cup (250g) fruit mince
¼ cup (20g) flaked almonds
2 teaspoons icing (confectioners') sugar

1 Preheat oven to 180°C/350°F. Grease 24cm x 32cm (9½-inch x 13-inch) swiss roll pan; line base and long sides with baking paper, extending paper 5cm (2 inches) over sides.
2 Beat butter and sugar in small bowl with electric mixer until light and fluffy. Beat in eggs, one at a time. Stir in sifted flours and milk. Spread mixture into pan; drop tablespoons of fruit mince over dough. Using the back of a spoon, swirl fruit mince through cake mixture; sprinkle with nuts.
3 Bake about 20 minutes. Dust with sifted icing sugar before cutting. Serve warm or at room temperature.

prep + cook time 30 minutes **makes** 20
tip We used fruit mince bought in a jar from the supermarket, but home-made would be even better.
Store squares in an airtight container for up to 3 days.

garibaldi slice

1½ cups (240g) currants
½ cup (80g) sultanas
½ cup (75g) raisins
½ cup (125ml) water
2 tablespoons dry sherry
1 egg, beaten lightly
2 tablespoons caster (superfine) sugar
pastry
2 cups (300g) plain (all-purpose) flour
⅓ cup (75g) caster (superfine) sugar
185g (6 ounces) cold butter, chopped coarsely
2 egg yolks
1 tablespoon iced water, approximately

1 Preheat oven to 180°C/350°F. Grease 24cm x 32cm (9½-inch x 13-inch) swiss roll pan.
2 Make pastry.
3 Combine fruit, the water and sherry in small saucepan; stir over low heat about 5 minutes or until liquid is absorbed and fruit soft. Blend or process fruit mixture until mixture is smooth. Cool.
4 Roll one portion of pastry between sheets of baking paper until large enough to line base of pan; lift pastry into pan, trimming to fit. Spread fruit mixture over pastry. Roll remaining pastry until large enough to cover fruit; lift pastry over fruit mixture, trimming to fit. Press down firmly. Cut top layer of pastry into 24 rectangles; prick each rectangle all over with a fork. Brush pastry with egg; sprinkle with sugar.
5 Bake about 30 minutes. Cool slice in pan before cutting.

pastry Sift flour and sugar into medium bowl; rub in butter. Stir in egg yolks and enough of the water to make a firm dough. Knead dough on floured surface until smooth. Divide dough in half; cover, refrigerate 30 minutes.

prep + cook time 50 minutes
(+ refrigeration)
makes 24
Store slice in an airtight container for up to 3 days.

plum and almond slice

825g (1¾ pounds) canned whole plums
in natural juice
2 star anise
1 cinnamon stick
1 tablespoon caster (superfine) sugar
185g (6 ounces) unsalted butter, softened
¾ cup (165g) caster (superfine) sugar, extra
1 teaspoon vanilla extract
3 eggs
1¾ cups (210g) ground almonds
1½ cups (225g) self-raising flour

1 Drain juice from plums into small saucepan; drain plums on absorbent paper. Add star anise, cinnamon and sugar to pan; bring to the boil. Boil, uncovered, until syrup is reduced by half. Cool 20 minutes. Cut plums in half; discard seeds.
2 Meanwhile, preheat oven to 160°C/325°F. Grease 24cm x 32cm (9½-inch x 13-inch) swiss roll pan; line base and long sides with baking paper, extending paper 5cm (2 inches) over sides.
3 Beat butter, extra sugar and extract in small bowl with electric mixer until light and fluffy. Beat in eggs, one at a time. Transfer mixture to large bowl; stir in ground almonds and sifted flour. Spread mixture into pan; top with plums, cut-side down.
4 Bake about 40 minutes. Stand slice in pan 10 minutes before turning onto wire rack to cool. Serve slice drizzled with syrup.

prep + cook time 55 minutes (+ cooling)
makes 48
Slice is best eaten on the day it is made.

strawberry and almond friand slice

6 egg whites
155g (5 ounces) unsalted butter, melted
2 tablespoons milk
1 teaspoon vanilla extract
1½ cups (180g) ground almonds
1½ cups (240g) icing (confectioners') sugar
½ cup (75g) self-raising flour
250g (8 ounces) strawberries, sliced thinly
⅓ cup (25g) flaked almonds
2 teaspoons icing (confectioners') sugar, extra

1 Preheat oven to 180°C/350°F. Grease 20cm x 30cm (8-inch x 12-inch) rectangular pan; line base and long sides with baking paper, extending paper 5cm (2 inches) over sides.
2 Place egg whites in medium bowl; whisk lightly with fork until combined. Add butter, milk, extract, ground almonds, sifted icing sugar and flour; stir until combined. Pour mixture into pan; top with berries.
3 Bake slice 15 minutes; remove from oven, sprinkle with nuts. Bake further 25 minutes. Stand slice in pan 10 minutes before turning onto a wire rack to cool. Dust the slice with sifted extra icing sugar before cutting.

prep + cook time 50 minutes **makes** 16
Store slice in an airtight container for up to 3 days.

cranberry and nut nougat slice

4 sheets confectioners' rice paper
2 tablespoons milk
20g (¾ ounce) butter
375g (12 ounces) white chocolate melts
410g (13 ounces) pink and white marshmallows,
    chopped coarsely
1 cup (130g) dried cranberries
½ cup (70g) unsalted shelled pistachios, roasted
½ cup (80g) blanched almonds, roasted

1 Grease 24cm x 32cm (9½-inch x 13-inch) swiss
roll pan; line base with 2 sheets of rice paper,
trimming to fit.
2 Combine milk, butter and melts in medium
heatproof bowl over medium saucepan of simmering
water; stir until smooth. Add marshmallows; stir
until smooth. Remove from heat; stir in cranberries
and nuts.
3 Spread mixture into pan; smooth surface. Top with
remaining rice paper, trimming to fit. Place a second
swiss roll pan on top of slice. Weight with cans;
refrigerate overnight.
4 Turn slice onto board before cutting.

prep + cook time 30 minutes (+ refrigeration)
makes 48
tip Rice paper is edible and ready to use. It can be
bought from specialty food stores; don't confuse this
paper with the rice paper used in recipes such as rice
paper rolls, which needs soaking to soften.
Store slice in an airtight container in the fridge for up
to a week.

marmalade, ginger and almond slice

90g (3 ounces) unsalted butter, softened
½ cup (110g) caster (superfine) sugar
1 egg
⅔ cup (100g) plain (all-purpose) flour
⅓ cup (50g) self-raising flour
1 cup (340g) orange marmalade
⅓ cup (60g) finely chopped glacé ginger
1 egg, beaten lightly, extra
1½ cups (120g) flaked almonds
½ cup (60g) ground almonds
1 tablespoon icing (confectioners') sugar

1 Preheat oven to 160°C/325°F. Grease 20cm x 30cm (8-inch x 12-inch) rectangular pan; line base and long sides with baking paper, extending paper 5cm (2 inches) over sides.
2 Beat butter, caster sugar and egg in small bowl with electric mixer until light and fluffy. Stir in sifted flours. Spread dough into pan. Combine marmalade and ginger in small bowl; spread over dough.
3 Combine extra egg, 1 cup (80g) of the flaked almonds and ground almonds in medium bowl. Spread almond mixture over marmalade; sprinkle with remaining nuts.
4 Bake about 40 minutes. Cool slice in pan. Dust with sifted icing sugar before cutting.

prep + cook time 1 hour
makes 24
Store slice in an airtight container for up to a week.

coconut cherry slice

395g (12½ ounces) canned sweetened
  condensed milk
155g (5 ounces) milk eating chocolate,
  chopped coarsely
⅓ cup (55g) icing (confectioners') sugar
⅓ cup (35g) cocoa powder
½ cup (100g) red glacé cherries, chopped finely
1½ cups (120g) desiccated coconut, toasted

1 Grease 20cm x 30cm (8-inch x 12-inch) rectangular
pan; line base and long sides with baking paper,
extending paper 5cm (2 inches) over sides.
2 Combine condensed milk, chocolate, sifted icing
sugar and cocoa in medium saucepan; stir over low
heat until smooth. Stir in cherries and 1⅓ cups (105g)
of the coconut. Spread mixture into pan, pressing
firmly; sprinkle with remaining coconut. Refrigerate
the slice 3 hours or overnight before cutting.

prep + cook time 20 minutes (+ refrigeration)
makes 50
tip Use a palette knife to press dough evenly over
base of pan.
Store slice in an airtight container for up to a week.

mixed spice fruit slice

2 cups (300g) plain (all-purpose) flour
⅓ cup (110g) icing (confectioners') sugar
250g (8 ounces) cold butter, chopped coarsely
2 teaspoons mixed spice
1 tablespoon caster (superfine) sugar
fruit filling
1 cup (140g) coarsely chopped seeded dried dates
1 cup (190g) coarsely chopped dried figs
½ cup (80g) currants

1 Preheat oven to 180°C/350°F. Grease 20cm x 30cm (8-inch x 12-inch) rectangular pan; line base and long sides with baking paper, extending paper 5cm (2 inches) over sides.
2 Process sifted flour and icing sugar, butter and spice until ingredients combine. Press half the dough into pan. Cover and refrigerate remaining dough. Bake 15 minutes, cool.
3 Meanwhile, make filling.
4 Using wet hand, press filling over base. Roll remaining dough between sheets of baking paper until large enough to cover filling; trim to fit. Brush dough with a little water; sprinkle with caster sugar.
5 Bake slice about 35 minutes. Cool slice in pan before cutting.

fruit filling Blend or process fruit until chopped finely.

prep + cook time 1 hour 20 minutes (+ refrigeration)
makes 16
tip Use a palette knife to press dough evenly over base of pan.
Store slice in an airtight container for up to a week.

caramelised pear and gingerbread slice

6 small pears (1.1kg)
60g (2 ounces) unsalted butter, chopped coarsely
¼ cup (55g) firmly packed light brown sugar
½ cup (175g) golden syrup or treacle
½ cup (125ml) water
⅓ cup (75g) firmly packed light brown sugar, extra
125g (4 ounces) unsalted butter, chopped
   coarsely, extra
1¾ cups (260g) plain (all-purpose) flour
½ teaspoon bicarbonate of soda (baking soda)
1 tablespoon ground ginger
½ teaspoon each ground nutmeg and cinnamon

1 Peel, quarter and core pears; halve quarters lengthways. Melt butter in large frying pan; add sugar and pears, turn pears. Cook over medium heat, turning occasionally, about 8 minutes or until pears are caramelised. Cool.
2 Meanwhile, preheat oven to 140°C/280°F. Grease 24cm x 32cm (9½-inch x 13-inch) swiss roll pan; line base and long sides with baking paper, extending paper 5cm (2 inches) over sides.
3 Combine syrup, the water, extra sugar and extra butter in medium saucepan; stir over low heat until mixture is smooth. Bring to the boil; remove from heat. Cool. Stir in sifted dry ingredients. Spread cake mixture into pan. Drain pears, gently push into cake mixture.
4 Bake slice about 30 minutes. Stand in pan 15 minutes before turning, pear-side up, onto wire rack to cool before cutting.

prep + cook time 1 hour (+ cooling & standing)
makes 16
tips We found the brown-skinned beurre bosc pears worked best for this recipe. Serve slice cold or warm as a dessert. It's delicious with a little crème fraîche or whipped cream.
Store slice in an airtight container in the fridge for up to 3 days.

chocolate and orange polenta squares

180g (6 ounces) dark eating (semi-sweet)
    chocolate, melted
½ cup (120g) sour cream
½ cup (110g) caster (superfine) sugar
90g (3 ounces) unsalted butter, softened
1 cup (150g) self-raising flour
½ cup (85g) polenta
⅓ cup (40g) ground almonds
2 teaspoons finely grated lemon rind
orange glaze
½ cup (80g) pure icing (confectioners') sugar
½ teaspoon finely grated orange rind
1 tablespoon orange juice

1 Preheat oven to 180°C/350°F. Grease 20cm x 30cm (8-inch x 12-inch) rectangular pan; line base and long sides with baking paper then a strip of foil, extending paper 5cm (2 inches) over sides.
2 Spread chocolate evenly over foil in base of pan. Refrigerate about 10 minutes or until set.
3 Meanwhile, beat sour cream, sugar and butter in small bowl with electric mixer until smooth and creamy. Add sifted flour and remaining ingredients. Beat on medium speed about 3 minutes or until mixture is changed to a paler colour; spread over chocolate.
4 Bake about 25 minutes. Cool slice in pan 10 minutes, then refrigerate about 30 minutes or until chocolate sets.
5 Make orange glaze.
6 Turn slice top side down onto board, carefully remove foil and paper from base. Turn slice top side up; spread slice with glaze. Refrigerate until set before cutting.

orange glaze Combine ingredients in small bowl.

prep + cook time 45 minutes (+ refrigeration)
makes 20
Store squares in an airtight container in the fridge for up to 3 days.

chewy pistachio and almond slice

1 cup (160g) blanched almonds, roasted
1 cup (140g) unsalted shelled pistachios, roasted
1½ cups (240g) icing (confectioners') sugar
1 egg
2 egg whites
green food colouring
1⅓ cups (110g) flaked almonds

1 Preheat oven to 170°C/340°F. Grease 20cm x 30cm (8-inch x 12-inch) rectangular pan; line base and long sides with baking paper, extending paper 5cm (2 inches) over sides.
2 Process blanched almonds and pistachios until fine. Combine nuts and sifted icing sugar in medium bowl; stir in egg and egg whites. Tint mixture green with colouring.
3 Sprinkle half the flaked almonds over base of pan. Drop spoonfuls of mixture over nuts; carefully spread mixture over nuts with a spatula. Sprinkle slice with remaining flaked almonds; press down firmly.
4 Bake about 30 minutes. Cool slice in pan before cutting.

prep + cook time 45 minutes **makes** 30
Store slice in an airtight container for up to a week.

hummingbird squares with cream cheese frosting

1 sheet shortcrust pastry
¾ cup (110g) self-raising flour
½ teaspoon each mixed spice
   and ground cinnamon
¼ teaspoon bicarbonate of soda (baking soda)
½ cup (110g) firmly packed light brown sugar
½ cup (40g) desiccated coconut
½ cup (50g) walnuts, chopped finely
½ cup mashed overripe banana
½ cup (130g) drained crushed pineapple
⅓ cup (80ml) vegetable oil
1 egg, beaten lightly
cream cheese frosting
250g (8 ounces) cream cheese, softened
½ cup (80g) icing (confectioners') sugar
2 teaspoons finely grated lemon rind

1 Preheat oven to 220°C/425°F. Grease 20cm x 30cm
(8-inch x 12-inch) rectangular pan; line base and long
sides with baking paper then a strip of foil, extending
paper 5cm (2 inches) over sides.
2 Trim pastry to fit base of pan; prick all over
with a fork. Bake 10 minutes. Cool. Reduce oven
temperature to 180°C/350°F.
3 Sift flour, spices and soda into large bowl; stir
in remaining ingredients. Spread mixture into pan;
smooth surface. Bake about 25 minutes. Cool
slice in pan.
4 Meanwhile, make cream cheese frosting. Spread
slice with frosting before cutting.

cream cheese frosting Beat ingredients in small
bowl with electric mixer until smooth.

prep + cook time 1 hour
makes 20
Store squares in an airtight container in the fridge for
up to 4 days.

albert squares

1 cup (160g) currants
125g (4 ounces) butter, softened
⅔ cup (150g) caster (superfine) sugar
1 tablespoon golden syrup or treacle
1 teaspoon vanilla extract
2 eggs
¾ cup (110g) plain (all-purpose) flour
¾ cup (110g) self-raising flour
½ cup (125ml) milk
1 cup (160g) icing (confectioners') sugar
1 teaspoon butter, softened, extra
1 tablespoon lemon juice, approximately
½ cup (40g) desiccated coconut

1 Preheat oven to 170°C/340°F. Grease 20cm x 30cm (8-inch x 12-inch) rectangular pan.
2 Rinse currants in sieve under warm water until water runs clear. Drain currants on absorbent paper; pat dry.
3 Beat butter, caster sugar, syrup and extract in small bowl with electric mixer until light and fluffy; beat in eggs, one at a time. Transfer mixture to large bowl; stir in sifted flours, milk and currants.
4 Spread mixture into pan; bake about 25 minutes.
5 Meanwhile, sift icing sugar into small bowl; stir in extra butter and enough of the juice to make a thick paste.
6 Spread icing over hot slice; sprinkle with coconut. Cool slice in pan before cutting.

prep + cook time 45 minutes **makes** 24
Store squares in an airtight container for up to 3 days.

glossary

ALMONDS flat, pointy-tipped nuts with a pitted brown shell enclosing a creamy white kernel which is covered by a brown skin.
blanched brown skins removed.
flaked paper-thin slices.
meal also known as ground almonds
slivered small pieces cut lengthways.

BAKING PAPER also known as parchment paper or baking parchment – is a silicone-coated paper that is primarily used for lining baking pans and oven trays so cakes and biscuits won't stick, making removal easy.

BAKING POWDER a raising agent consisting mainly of two parts cream of tartar to one part bicarbonate of soda.

BEURRE BOSC PEARS this firm and crunchy pear is the best choice for cooking, because it holds its shape nicely. Available from greengrocers and supermarkets.

BICARBONATE OF SODA (BAKING SODA) an acid and alkaline combination, which when moistened and heated, gives off carbon dioxide that aerates and lightens the mixture during baking.

BISCUITS also known as cookies.
butternut snap crunchy cookie made with golden syrup, oats and coconut.
gingernuts a plain biscuit made with golden syrup and ginger. Comes in soft and hard varieties; available from supermarkets.
shortbread plain buttery biscuit with a crumbly texture.
BUTTER we use salted butter unless stated otherwise; 125g is equal to 1 stick (4 ounces).

CASHEWS plump, kidney-shaped, golden-brown nuts with a distinctive sweet, buttery flavour and containing about 48 per cent fat. Because of this high fat content, they should be kept, sealed tightly, under refrigeration to avoid becoming rancid.

CHOCOLATE
choc bits also known as chocolate chips or chocolate morsels; available in milk, white and dark chocolate. They hold their shape in baking and are ideal for decorating.
couverture a term used to describe a fine quality, very rich chocolate high in both cocoa butter and cocoa liquor. Requires tempering when used to coat but not if used in baking, mousses or fillings.
dark eating also known as semi-sweet or luxury chocolate; made of a high percentage of cocoa liquor and cocoa butter, and little added sugar. Unless stated otherwise, we use dark eating chocolate in this book as it's ideal for use in desserts and cakes.
milk most popular eating chocolate, mild and very sweet; similar in make-up to dark with the difference being the addition of milk solids.
white contains no cocoa solids but derives its sweet flavour from cocoa butter. Very sensitive to heat.

CINNAMON available both in the piece (called sticks or quills) and ground into powder; one of the world's most common spices, used universally as a sweet, fragrant flavouring for both sweet and savoury foods. The dried inner bark of the shoots of the Sri Lankan native cinnamon tree; much of what is sold as the real thing is in fact cassia, chinese cinnamon, from the bark of the cassia tree. Less expensive to process than true cinnamon, it is often blended with sri lankan cinnamon to produce the "cinnamon" most commonly found.

CINNAMON SUGAR a combination of ground cinnamon and caster sugar. It is available from supermarkets in the spice section.

COCO POPS chocolate-flavoured puffed rice breakfast cereal.

COCOA POWDER also known as unsweetened cocoa; cocoa beans (cacao seeds) that have been fermented, roasted, shelled, ground into powder then cleared of most of the fat content.

COCONUT
desiccated concentrated, dried, unsweetened, finely shredded coconut.
shredded unsweetened thin strips of dried coconut flesh.

CONFECTIONERS' RICE PAPER is made from a dough made from the pith of an Asian shrub called the rice-paper plant (or rice-paper tree), not from rice. It resembles a grainy sheet of paper and is used in confectionery and baking. It can be bought from specialty food stores; don't confuse it with the rice paper used in recipes such as Asian rice paper rolls, which needs soaking to soften.

CORN FLAKES breakfast cereal made of dehydrated then baked crisp flakes of corn.

CORN SYRUP, LIGHT an imported product available in some supermarkets, delicatessens and health food stores. Made from cornstarch, it is a popular ingredient in American cooking for frostings, jams and jellies.

CORNFLOUR also known as cornstarch. Available made from corn or wheat (wheaten cornflour gives a lighter texture in cakes); used as a thickening agent in cooking.

CRANBERRIES fruit available dried and frozen; have a rich, astringent flavour and can be used in cooking sweet and savoury dishes. The dried version can usually be substituted for or with other dried fruit.

CREAM we used fresh cream, also known as pure or pouring cream unless otherwise stated. It contains no additives and has a minimum fat content of 35 per cent.
sour a thick commercially cultured soured cream with a minimum fat content of 35 per cent.
thick (double) a dolloping cream with a minimum fat content of 45 per cent.
thickened (heavy) a whipping cream containing thickener. Minimum fat content of 35 per cent.

CREAM CHEESE commonly called philadelphia or philly; a soft cow's milk cheese, its fat content ranges from 14 to 33 per cent.

CREAM OF TARTAR the acid

ingredient in baking powder; added to confectionery mixtures to help prevent sugar from crystallising. Keeps frostings creamy and improves volume when beating egg whites.

CREME FRAICHE a mature, naturally fermented cream (minimum fat content 35 per cent) with a velvety texture and slightly tangy, nutty flavour. This French variation of sour cream can boil without curdling and be used in sweet and savoury dishes.

CURRANTS, DRIED tiny, almost black raisins so-named after a grape that originated in Corinth, Greece.

CUSTARD POWDER instant powdered mixture used to make pouring custard; similar to North American instant pudding mixes.

EGGS we use large chicken eggs weighing an average of 60g unless stated otherwise in the recipes in this book. If a recipe calls for raw or barely cooked eggs, exercise caution if there is a salmonella problem in your area, particularly in food eaten by children and pregnant women.

EXTRACT/ESSENCE an essence is either a distilled concentration of a food quality or an artificial creation of it. An extract is made by extracting the flavour from a food product. Essences and extracts keep indefinitely if stored in a cool dark place.

FLOUR
plain also known as all-purpose; unbleached wheat flour is the best for baking: the gluten content ensures a strong dough and a light result.
potato is made from cooked potatoes that have been dried and ground into fine flour.
rice a very fine flour, made from ground rice.
self-raising all-purpose plain or wholemeal flour with baking powder and salt added; make yourself with plain or wholemeal flour sifted with baking powder in the proportion of 1 cup flour to 2 teaspoons baking powder.

FRUIT MINCE also known as mincemeat. A mixture of dried fruits such as raisins, sultanas and candied peel, nuts, spices, apple, brandy or rum. Is used as a filling for cakes, puddings and fruit mince pies.

GELATINE we use dried (powdered) gelatine in this book; it's also available in sheet form known as leaf gelatine. A thickening agent made from either collagen, a protein found in animal connective tissue and bones, or certain algae (agar-agar). Three teaspoons of dried gelatine (8g or one sachet) is about the same as four gelatine leaves. The two types are interchangable but leaf gelatine gives a much clearer mixture than dried gelatine; it's perfect in dishes where appearance matters.

GLACE CHERRIES or candied cherries; boiled in heavy sugar syrup then dried.

GLACÉ GINGER fresh ginger root preserved in sugar syrup; crystallised ginger (sweetened with cane sugar) can be substituted if rinsed with warm water and dried before using.

GLUCOSE SYRUP also known as liquid glucose, made from wheat starch; used in jam and confectionery and available at health food stores and supermarkets.

GOLDEN SYRUP a by-product of refined sugarcane; pure maple syrup or honey can be substituted. Treacle is more viscous, and has a stronger flavour and aroma than golden syrup (which has been refined further and contains fewer impurities, so is lighter in colour and more fluid).

GROUND GINGER also called powdered ginger; used as a flavouring in baking but cannot be substituted for fresh ginger.

HAZELNUTS also known as filberts; plump, grape-sized, rich, sweet nut having a brown skin that is removed by rubbing heated nuts together vigorously in a tea-towel. Hazelnut meal is made by grounding the hazelnuts to a coarse flour texture for use in baking or as a thickening agent.

HONEY the variety sold in a squeezable container is not suitable for the recipes in this book.

JAM also known as preserve or conserve; most often made from fruit.

LOLLIES a confectionery also known as sweets or candy.

MACADAMIAS native to Australia; fairly large, slightly soft, buttery rich nut. Used to make oil and macadamia butter; equally good in salads or cakes and pastries; delicious eaten on their own. Should always be stored in the fridge to prevent their high oil content turning them rancid.

MAPLE SYRUP distilled from the sap of sugar maple trees found only in Canada and about ten states in the USA. Most often eaten with pancakes or waffles, but also used as an ingredient in baking or in preparing desserts. Maple-flavoured syrup or pancake syrup is not an adequate substitute for the real thing.

MARMALADE a preserve, usually based on citrus fruit.

MARSALA a fortified Italian wine produced in the region surrounding the Sicilian city of Marsala.

MARSHMALLOWS pink and white; made from sugar, glucose, gelatine and cornflour.

MASCARPONE CHEESE an Italian fresh cultured-cream product made in much the same way as yogurt. Whiteish to creamy yellow in colour, with a buttery-rich, luscious texture. Soft, creamy and spreadable, it is used in Italian desserts and as an accompaniment to fresh fruit.

MILK we use full-cream homogenised milk unless otherwise specified.
buttermilk in spite of its name, buttermilk is actually low in fat, varying between 0.6 per cent and 2.0 per cent per 100ml. Originally the term given to the slightly sour liquid left after butter was churned from cream, today it is intentionally made from no-fat or low-fat milk to which specific bacterial cultures have been added during the

manufacturing process. It is readily available from the dairy department in supermarkets. Because it is low in fat, it's a good substitute for dairy products such as cream or sour cream in some baking and salad dressings.

evaporated unsweetened canned milk from which water has been extracted by evaporation. Evaporated skim or low-fat milk has 0.3 per cent fat content.

full-cream powder instant powdered milk made from whole cow milk with liquid removed and emulsifiers added.

sweetened condensed a canned milk product consisting of milk with more than half the water content removed and sugar added to the remaining milk.

MIXED DRIED FRUIT a combination of sultanas, raisins, currants, mixed peel and cherries.

MIXED SPICE a classic spice mixture generally containing caraway, allspice, coriander, cumin, nutmeg and ginger, although cinnamon and other spices can be added. It is used with fruit and in cakes.

MUESLI also known as granola, a combination of grains (mainly oats), nuts and dried fruits. Some manufacturers toast their product in oil and honey, adding crispness and kilojoules.

NUTMEG a strong and pungent spice ground from the dried nut of an evergreen tree native to Indonesia. Usually found ground but the flavour is more intense from a whole nut, available from spice shops, so it's best to grate your own.

NOUGAT a popular confection in southern Europe; made from sugar or honey, roasted nuts, sometimes candied fruits and beaten egg white (for soft nougat) or caramelised sugar (for hard nougat).

PEANUTS also known as groundnut, not in fact a nut but the pod of a legume. We mainly use raw (unroasted) or unsalted roasted peanuts.

PEANUT BUTTER peanuts ground to a paste; available in crunchy and smooth varieties.

PECANS native to the US and now grown locally; pecans are golden brown, buttery and rich. Walnuts are a good substitute.

PISTACHIOS green, delicately flavoured nuts inside hard off-white shells. Available salted or unsalted in their shells; you can also buy shelled.

POLENTA also known as cornmeal; a flour-like cereal made of dried corn (maize). Also the dish made from it.

POPCORN a variety of corn that is sold as kernels for popping corn, or can be bought ready popped.

RAISINS dried sweet grapes (traditionally muscatel grapes).

RHUBARB a plant with long, green-red stalks; becomes edible when cooked.

READY-MADE WHITE ICING also known as soft icing, ready-to-roll and prepared fondant.

RICE BUBBLES a small puffed rice breakfast cereal.

ROLLED OATS flattened oat grain rolled into flakes and traditionally used for porridge. Instant oats are also available, but we prefer to use traditional oats for baking.

SEMOLINA coarsely ground flour milled from durum wheat; it's the flour that's used in making gnocchi, pasta and couscous.

SHERRY fortified wine consumed as an aperitif or used in cooking. Sold as fino (light, dry), amontillado (medium sweet, dark) and oloroso (full-bodied, very dark).

SUGAR we use coarse, granulated table sugar, also known as crystal sugar, unless otherwise specified.

brown a soft, finely granulated sugar retaining molasses for its characteristic colour and flavour.

caster also known as superfine or finely granulated table sugar.

demerara small-grained golden-coloured crystal sugar.

icing also known as confectioners' sugar or powdered sugar; pulverised granulated sugar crushed together with a small amount of cornflour.

muscovado a fine-grained, moist sugar that comes in two types, light and dark. Light muscovado has a light toffee flavour and is good for sticky toffee sauce and caramel ice-cream. Dark muscovado is used in sauces.

palm also called nam tan pip, jaggery, jawa or gula melaka; made from the sap of the sugar palm tree. Light brown to black in colour and usually sold in rock-hard cakes; use with brown sugar if unavailable.

pure icing also known as confectioners' sugar or powdered sugar.

raw natural brown granulated sugar.

SULTANAS dried sweet grapes of the sultana variety.

STAR ANISE a dried star-shaped pod with seeds with an astringent aniseed flavour; commonly used to flavour stocks and marinades.

VANILLA

bean dried, long, thin pod from a tropical golden orchid; the minuscule black seeds inside the bean are used to impart a luscious vanilla flavour in baking and desserts. Place a whole bean in a jar of sugar to make the vanilla sugar often called for in recipes; a bean can be used three or four times.

extract obtained from vanilla beans infused in water; a non-alcoholic version of essence.

WALNUTS as well as being a good source of fibre and healthy oils, nuts contain a range of vitamins, minerals and other beneficial plant components called phytochemicals. Walnuts contain the beneficial omega-3 fatty acids.

WEET-BIX also known as ruskets; wholewheat malted breakfast biscuit.

YOGURT we use plain full-cream yogurt in our recipes unless specifically noted otherwise. If a recipe in this book calls for low-fat yogurt, we use one with a fat content of less than 0.2 per cent.

conversion chart

MEASURES

One Australian metric measuring cup holds approximately 250ml; one Australian metric tablespoon holds 20ml; one Australian metric teaspoon holds 5ml.

The difference between one country's measuring cups and another's is within a two- or three-teaspoon variance, and will not affect your cooking results. North America, New Zealand and the United Kingdom use a 15ml tablespoon.

All cup and spoon measurements are level. The most accurate way of measuring dry ingredients is to weigh them. When measuring liquids, use a clear glass or plastic jug with the metric markings.

We use large eggs with an average weight of 60g.

DRY MEASURES

METRIC	IMPERIAL
15g	½oz
30g	1oz
60g	2oz
90g	3oz
125g	4oz (¼lb)
155g	5oz
185g	6oz
220g	7oz
250g	8oz (½lb)
280g	9oz
315g	10oz
345g	11oz
375g	12oz (¾lb)
410g	13oz
440g	14oz
470g	15oz
500g	16oz (1lb)
750g	24oz (1½lb)
1kg	32oz (2lb)

LIQUID MEASURES

METRIC	IMPERIAL
30ml	1 fluid oz
60ml	2 fluid oz
100ml	3 fluid oz
125ml	4 fluid oz
150ml	5 fluid oz
190ml	6 fluid oz
250ml	8 fluid oz
300ml	10 fluid oz
500ml	16 fluid oz
600ml	20 fluid oz
1000ml (1 litre)	1¾ pints

LENGTH MEASURES

METRIC	IMPERIAL
3mm	⅛in
6mm	¼in
1cm	½in
2cm	¾in
2.5cm	1in
5cm	2in
6cm	2½in
8cm	3in
10cm	4in
13cm	5in
15cm	6in
18cm	7in
20cm	8in
23cm	9in
25cm	10in
28cm	11in
30cm	12in (1ft)

OVEN TEMPERATURES

The oven temperatures in this book are for conventional ovens; if you have a fan-forced oven, decrease the temperature by 10-20 degrees.

	°C (CELSIUS)	°F (FAHRENHEIT)
Very slow	120	250
Slow	150	300
Moderately slow	160	325
Moderate	180	350
Moderately hot	200	400
Hot	220	425
Very hot	240	475

The imperial measurements used in these recipes are approximate only. Measurements for cake pans are approximate only. Using same-shaped cake pans of a similar size should not affect the outcome of your baking. We measure the inside top of the cake pan to determine sizes.

index

First published in 2011 by ACP Magazines Ltd,
a division of Nine Entertainment Co.
54 Park St, Sydney
GPO Box 4088, Sydney, NSW 2001.
phone (02) 9282 8618; fax (02) 9267 9438
acpbooks@acpmagazines.com.au; www.acpbooks.com.au

ACP BOOKS
General Manager · Christine Whiston
Associate publisher · Seymour Cohen
Editor-in-Chief · Susan Tomnay
Creative Director · Hieu Chi Nguyen
Food Director · Pamela Clark

Published and Distributed in the United Kingdom by Octopus Publishing Group
Endeavour House
189 Shaftesbury Avenue
London WC2H 8JY
United Kingdom
phone (+44)(0)207 632 5400; fax (+44)(0)207 632 5405
info@octopus-publishing.co.uk;
www.octopusbooks.co.uk

Printed by Toppan Printing Co., China

International foreign language rights, Brian Cearnes, ACP Books bcearnes@acpmagazines.com.au

A catalogue record for this book is available from the British Library.
ISBN 978-1-74245-059-9 (pbk.)
© ACP Magazines Ltd 2011
ABN 18 053 273 546